500
TIPS
for
TESOL

500 Tips from Routledgefalmer

500 TIPS

for

TESOL

(TEACHING ENGLISH TO SPEAKERS
OF OTHER LANGUAGES)

SUE WHARTON
& PHIL RACE

RoutledgeFalmer
Taylor & Francis Group

LONDON AND NEW YORK

First published in 1999 by Routledgefalmer

Reprinted 2004
by Routledgefalmer
2 Park Square, Milton Park, Abingdon, Oxon, OX14 4RN

Transferred to Digital Printing 2006

RoutledgeFalmer is an imprint of the Taylor & Francis Group

British Library Cataloguing in Publication Data

A CIP record for this book is available from the British Library.

ISBN 0 7494 2409 5

Typeset by Jo Brereton, Primary Focus, Haslington, Cheshire

Contents

v

Acknowledgements

We would like to thank Fiona Copland, Julian Edge, Nur Hooton, Steve Mann, Kate Marriage, Peter Roe, Ann Wharton, Shana Heslington and Jane Willis for their extremely valuable comments on earlier drafts of all or part of this book. We also thank participants on Aston University's CELT course who used and commented on draft extracts from the book. The responsibility for any errors which remain is entirely our own.

Introduction

We have written this book for people who teach English to speakers of other languages, for people who are training to do so, and for people who work with trainee teachers. Although it is primarily intended for those nearer the beginning of their careers, it will also be of use to more experienced teachers who are moving into new areas, such as course design, self-access provision or teacher training. So, whether you are just starting your career or whether you have been teaching for a long time now, we hope you will find useful suggestions in our book.

Chapter 1, 'Planning for teaching and learning', starts by exploring the basis of successful learning processes. We look at the assessment of learners' needs, from both a language learning and a more broadly human perspective, and then go on to look at planning a course and locating and designing suitable materials to support it.

Chapter 2, 'Meeting learners' needs', looks in more depth at language learners as social human beings. We consider how to foster valuable learning processes in the classroom, and offer practical tips on how to handle large groups and smaller groups. We also make suggestions on how best to support mature learners, and learners away from home. We end with a discussion of ways of collecting useful feedback from the learners themselves.

Chapter 3 is the most substantial part of this book and deals with a range of language teaching activities. We look first at techniques for teaching the various aspects of language, and end with some ideas about creative things, such as games and role plays, that can contribute to the learning of a wide range of content and skills.

Chapter 4 is about using flexible or self-access learning in your work, or even to replace well-chosen aspects of your normal face-to-face provision. We look at the establishment of self-access facilities, their use, and the choice and design of materials to go in them.

Chapter 5 offers suggestions on ways of making use of information and communications technologies to support ESOL learning. The use of e-mail and computer conferencing can be particularly useful to people learning a language, giving them practice in a non-threatening environment, both at reading and writing in their target language.

Chapter 6 is about assessment, including helping learners to benefit from self-assessment and peer-assessment. The chapter includes suggestions for helping learners to prepare successfully for public examinations.

Chapter 7 is written for you! We include various suggestions from which to choose your own personal professional development activities, and also some 'survival' suggestions, which we hope will prove useful to you if and when they are needed.

This is not a book to be read straight through from start to finish. We suggest that you scan the book to find out what is most directly relevant to you at any given time, and start from there. If you are an experienced teacher, we know that you may already be implementing, or exceeding, many of the suggestions we offer; but we hope that you will still find ideas that you had not considered before, and which you can adapt to your own teaching. If you are a new teacher, we realize that not all of our suggestions may be immediately relevant to you; we hope that you will take those that you need now (Chapter 3 might be a good place to start), and come back later to some of the others. Then if you are training teachers, we hope that these sets of tips will be useful springboards to discussion in training sessions or reminders afterwards.

At the end of the book we include suggestions for further reading for all of the chapters. These books and articles will help you to look in much more detail at all of the areas which we have touched on in this book. We've chosen titles that we feel will be accessible to less experienced teachers, but which will also provide more experienced colleagues with food for thought.

Chapter 1 Planning for Teaching and Learning

We begin the book by looking at the key processes that underpin and drive successful learning. We hope that our suggestions will help you to plan your programmes so that the learning experiences your learners derive are as productive as possible, as well as being enjoyable and stimulating.

Next, we look at your market research. The more you can find out about *why* your learners are learning English, and *what* they intend to do with their new language, the better you can plan your programme for them.

There is a lot more to planning a course than can realistically be covered in a few suggestions. We hope, however, that our ideas on this will point you in productive directions, will include at least one or two ideas which you may not otherwise have considered, and will help you to make the process of course design more worthwhile, and the resulting product more useful.

If you intend your students' learning to be supported by a particular coursebook, it is obvious that you need to select the most appropriate book, so that your learners' needs will be met well, and also that you will find it a resource with which is comfortable to work.

We end this short chapter with some general suggestions about designing your own materials. Every teacher we know, even when making extensive use of published materials, finds it necessary to make materials of their own to cover particular issues. Later in this book, we revisit materials issues in the context of choosing or designing resource materials for independent learning.

1

Exploring learning processes

One of the most important factors that predetermines success in learning of any kind is confidence. Language learning is particularly dependent upon confidence. We need to give our learners every chance to develop this confidence, and one of the best ways of us assisting them to do this is to help them to gain greater control over the processes they apply during their learning. The following ideas should help you to show your learners how they can adjust their approaches to learning to optimize their success.

1   **Learners need motivation.** They need to want to learn things. If they already want to learn, it is described as intrinsic motivation. Where intrinsic motivation is lacking, you can encourage learners by showing them what benefits will flow from the achievement of their intended learning outcomes. This generates extrinsic motivation. When possible, make learning fun, interesting and rewarding, so that extrinsic and intrinsic motivation can work together. Don't mistake lack of confidence for lack of motivation.

2   **Learning-by-doing is important.** Most learning happens when learners use language, have a go, and learn by making mistakes and finding out why. We need to ensure that learners are given early opportunities to try out and work with new language that they have encountered. Care needs to be taken to ensure that learning-by-doing is focused on *useful* language work, and not just on anything to keep learners busy!

3   **Feedback to learners is essential.** They need to find out how their learning is actually going. They may feel that they have understood a particular aspect of language, but cannot be certain until they get feedback on whether they are handling it successfully. Feedback from the teacher is very useful, but teachers can also facilitate learners getting feedback from each other, and from various kinds of learning resource materials. It follows, too, that feedback must be timely for it to be of use to the learner. Any significant delay in the return of an assessed piece of written work usually causes gloom and distress!

4   **Needing to learn something can be almost as productive as wanting to learn it.** When learners know *why* something will be useful to them, even if they find it difficult, they are more likely to maintain their efforts until they have succeeded.

5   **Learners need to make sense of what they are learning.** It is of limited value to learn only by rote, or to be able to do things without knowing why or how. Getting learners to think about how their learning is happening is one step towards helping them to develop a sense of ownership of their progress.

6   **Learning is not just a matter of storing up further knowledge.** Successful learning, especially language learning, is about being able to make creative use of what has been learnt, not only in familiar situations, but also in new contexts. It is essential to keep in mind the need to help students to learn in both sequential and holistic ways, and to look for ways to help them to employ all of their senses to optimize their learning.

7   **Learners take cues about how they are expected to learn from the ways in which we teach them.** If we concentrate only on supplying them with information, they are likely to simply try to store this. If we structure our teaching so that they are practising, applying, extending, comparing, contrasting, evaluating and engaging in other higher level processes, they are likely to see these processes as central to their learning.

8   **Learning is driven strongly by assessment.** Learners are often quite strategic in structuring their learning to be able to do the best they can in the contexts in which their learning is to be assessed. Assessment formats and instruments can be used to help learners to structure their learning effectively, as well as to give them appropriate timescales within which to organize their learning.

9   **Learning is not just an independent activity.** While much can be learnt by learners working on their own, with handouts, books and learning resource materials, they can also learn a great deal by talking to each other and attempting tasks and activities jointly.

10   **Becoming better at learning is important.** For many people, the most important learning outcomes of an educational experience are not the syllabus-based, course-specific ones, but are the outcomes relating to being able to learn new skills and competencies better. Learning skills are among the most important of transferable life skills. The course content can be regarded as a vehicle through which these important skills are developed.

2

Assessing learners' language needs

It seems only common sense to try to find out what our learners are learning English for and what kind of English they will need. Many will have no specific purpose in mind, but others – usually adults – are learning for clearly identified reasons: to study at an English medium university; to read the literature of their professional field; to work with English speakers. If you have a class with learning purposes in common, you can try to tailor your course to their particular language needs. The following suggestions should help you to find out, in detail, what those language needs are.

1   **Ask learners about their reasons for learning and their target situation.** If you ask a very general, open-ended question then learners can tell you about their needs in their own words. You will gain insight into the level of sophistication at which they can express their language needs, and the extent to which they are aware of a target language variety.

2   **Ask people who are already in the target situation.** These may be people who already occupy the roles your learners aspire to, or people like managers and trainers who may be evaluating the performance of your learners in their target roles. People already in the situation will have a valuable perspective on its demands; but, just like the learners, they may have limited awareness of actual language needs.

3   **Observe the target situation first hand.** When trying to understand your learners' aspirations there is no substitute for actually observing the kind of activities they want to carry out in English and the environment that they will be in. Sometimes, it is only seeing for yourself that enables the comments of the learners and other informants to make sense.

4 **Talk to learners again, in detail.** Once you have a broad picture of the target situation, you can talk to learners about those aspects of it which might particularly influence the ways they want to use language. The following tips suggest areas that you might concentrate on.

5 **Clarify receptive and productive needs.** Language needs are defined by what users do with language in situations, as much as by the language which they encounter. For example, your learners may need to understand the financial press, but never have to produce such language themselves. Getting this clear will help you to develop relevant and economical teaching approaches.

6 **Find out about the cognitive demands of situations.** For example, if your learners say they need to 'understand lectures', find out why this is: will they write summaries, undertake tasks, sit exams on the basis of what they have learnt from lectures? This information can give you ideas both on skills to practise (eg, taking notes), and on language to highlight (eg, discourse markers).

7 **Ask about social roles.** If your learners need to 'give presentations', is this to peers, juniors or potential clients? Social considerations are particularly important for classroom activities, such as role plays: you need to think about how social dimensions can be recreated or simulated in the classroom, so that learners might attempt to incorporate a degree of social positioning into their classroom language use.

8 **Research the target language yourself.** Try to get a good range of samples – written and spoken, as appropriate – and look at them in detail. You will perhaps be able to identify certain language features that you feel are particularly important, and which you want to incorporate into your course. For more ideas on collecting and analyzing language data, see 21 on natural language data, and 22–23 on exploiting written and spoken texts.

9 **Look at how your learners will be tested.** Sometimes, learners need to take a language test to gain access to their target role: eg, TOEFL or IELTS for university study. In this case, the nature of the test is one of the factors determining their language needs. See 42, Preparing learners for public examinations.

10   **Remember that language needs aren't everything.** There is a danger of getting so caught up in attempting to understand, express and itemize the language needs of students that we start to lose sight of their needs as learners and human beings. Learning needs, as distinct from language needs, are discussed from a variety of perspectives in Chapter 2 of this book.

3

Planning a course

Teachers are often asked to work with a course plan that already exists. This may be an explicit document generated within the institution, or a more implicit statement such as a prescribed coursebook. But, sometimes, individual teachers or groups of colleagues need to plan a course themselves. These suggestions should help you to plan a coherent learning experience for your students.

1   **Know your learners.** A prerequisite for course planning is an analysis of learners' needs, in terms of both language content and skills and learning processes. Good needs analysis involves a process of research – we provide ideas on how to carry it out in 2, Assessing learners' language needs, and 6, Responding to learning needs in the classroom.

2   **Formulate aims and objectives**. On the basis of your research, what do you want the learners to be able to do by the end of the course? What do you want them to have read and listened to? How can these objectives be broken down into manageable steps?

3   **Name the strands of the learning experience.** These are the means whereby the objectives might be reached. You should consider processes (eg, the tasks learners might do), topics and text types as well as language content. Having named the strands, you can then consider each one in detail – examples are below.

4   **Consider the language content.** You may well be required to specify the main structures, lexis and language functions that learners will experience and work with during the course. You should link these features to the overall aims and objectives of your course. In addition to their experience of these explicitly stated language features, learners need a general variety of exposure – to give them opportunities to acquire features which are not being explicitly taught. So don't overlook the importance of language and texts that do *not* relate directly to course objectives.

5   **Think about topics and text types.** Do the course objectives imply a concentration on particular topics and written or spoken text types? Are some topics particularly relevant and interesting for the learners? Which text types might most easily support the language content objectives, as well as contributing to a wide exposure?

6   **Think about processes.** Is familiarity with certain processes – for example, negotiating in a group, or writing a summary from various source texts – part of the course objectives? Perhaps your learners can already identify some of the activities they need to perform in English. Which processes do you think will best support your language content objectives? Which will best support the students' general language learning?

7   **Decide on a sequence for the course elements.** You need a rationale that will help you to determine which aspects will come first, which later, and how aspects will be recycled. You might think of immediate need, relevance, or difficulty. The concept of difficulty here is, of course, a complex one, and begs questions about what can be meant by 'mastery' of a course element.

8   **Get feedback on your draft course.** Especially where one person or a small group is planning a course that will also be used by others, it is essential to get feedback from those others before the course plan is finalized. Colleagues can spot problems, from gaps in course coverage to ambiguous or difficult formulations. And the process of consultation makes it more likely that all the team will understand the philosophy of the course and engage with it.

9   **Develop a formal, public document.** The 'finished' course document or course description can be made available not only to teachers using it, but also to other colleagues, learners, sponsors and parents. Writing for so many different audiences is a challenge, but a document that successfully addresses all stakeholders can be a powerful unifying force.

10   **Remain open to change.** As the course is taught, experiences of teachers and learners will no doubt start to reveal ways in which it could be improved. You need to set up a system to channel these developing insights back to you. It could well be impractical, as well as inappropriate, to radically change the course plan every year; but do remain open to feedback and modifications.

4

Choosing the right coursebook

A good coursebook makes a tremendous difference to a programme. For learners, it can give confidence and reassurance, as well as the opportunity to look ahead and see what's coming next. For teachers, it offers a framework for course planning as well as lesson-by-lesson support. Sometimes we are told which book to use; but often, individual teachers or groups of colleagues are asked to choose a main book for their programme. The following suggestions should help you to evaluate potential coursebooks and choose the best one for your learners.

1   **Get a clear picture of your students' language learning needs.** Then see how well the coursebook matches them. Is the emphasis on grammar, vocabulary, pronunciation etc appropriate? What about the balance of skills work? Also, consider the language used for dialogues and listening/reading passages: is it the kind of language your learners are aiming to understand and use?

2   **Examine the syllabus organization.** Contents pages usually make it clear whether the book is primarily organized according to a structural, functional, lexical or indeed a multi-syllabus. They also show how much new content there is in each unit, and the extent to which new language is recycled throughout the book. How does the book's approach fit with your own objectives for your course?

3   **Think about how your students want to learn.** Ask yourself whether the methodology suggested by the coursebook is in fact appropriate for them. Are the roles suggested for teachers and learners ones that your own learners will be used to? Will the activities be reasonably familiar? You will need to think about socio-cultural habits and preferences here, as well as about successful language learning.

4   **Examine the subject content of the book.** Language learning is part of a wider educational experience, and the thematic content of a coursebook should be considered from this perspective. A book should provide stimulation and cognitive challenge, without causing bewilderment or offence. This can be a difficult balance to strike when books are written in one cultural context and used in another.

5   **Think about the kind of classroom interactions you want to have.** Find out whether the book is likely to provide them. For example, how much time might your learners like to spend working individually? In pairs or groups? As a whole class? And what sort of tasks would they get most benefit from? By looking at the activities suggested in the coursebook, you will see how your learners might be relating to each other as they use it.

6   **Consider your own needs as a teacher.** Coursebooks are usually accompanied by teachers' guides, which vary a great deal in the level of support they provide. Ask yourself whether you can empathize with the advice given in the teachers' guide, and what you can learn from it. Will you feel comfortable adopting the roles the teachers' guide suggests for you?

7   **Consider the needs of your institution.** Coursebooks usually come as part of a package that includes teachers' guide, workbooks, cassettes, video... if not more. Is your institution able and willing to purchase all of these? If not, you will need to assess whether the coursebook is in fact usable without all the other elements of the package. You should also consider how long your new purchases will be expected to last!

8   **Work with colleagues to choose your coursebook.** Where a book is being chosen for a whole teaching team, it is important for all colleagues to be involved. That way everyone's needs can be considered, and the whole team has ownership of the final decision. But even if you are choosing a book just for your own class, discussion with colleagues is beneficial: it forces you to be explicit about your own criteria, and may provide perspectives you haven't yet considered.

9   **Ask your learners about their criteria for a good coursebook.** This will give you a useful picture of their priorities. The process will also be of benefit to them, because they will reflect about what helps them with their learning. You may find you get more useful feedback by asking a reasonably structured series of questions.

10   **Whatever evaluation techniques you use, keep your own situation firmly in mind.** There are no inherently good or inherently bad coursebooks, only coursebooks which are better or worse in particular situations. Make sure any evaluation you undertake reflects your own priorities.

5

Designing your own materials

Despite the excellent range of published materials available, and all the options that we have for flexible use of these, there are still occasions when teachers need or prefer to make their own materials. The following suggestions will help you make the most of whatever resources you have available to create materials that will enhance your students' learning experience.

1   **Take care over the appearance of your materials.** Not everyone has access to desktop publishing software and laser printers, but we can all make good use of layout, white space and print sizes to make our materials look attractive. By taking care over your materials, you show learners that you have a serious attitude to preparing for the class.

2   **Give your materials a house identity.** Heading all your materials with the name or logo of your institution, course or class gives them a more 'official' stamp and is another encouragement for learners to take them seriously. Learners are more likely to file numbered, titled handouts than odd sheets of paper!

3   **Have clear objectives for the materials.** If you push yourself to say explicitly what your objectives are, it is more likely that you will be able to develop materials that are relevant to your learners' needs and to the objectives of your course. As you write the materials, the objectives are a reference point to make sure your materials stay on task.

4   **Choose source material carefully.** Your materials will probably be designed around some sort of written or spoken source text. Make sure this is appropriate for the learners in terms of topic and level – and that it lends itself to an exploitation that is relevant to your learners' needs and the objectives of the course.

5   **Design appropriate tasks.** The tasks in your materials need to be appropriate to your course objectives and your learners' interests. They should also be manageable within the time frame you have available. Learners should enjoy them in their own right and/or be able to see why they are important for a future goal.

6   **Include clear rubrics.** Almost all materials include instructions to the learners, and those you make for your own class should not be an exception. Especially for a complex series of tasks, learners can find it reassuring to see all the steps written down in the materials.

7   **Make the materials personally relevant to the learners.** Designing your own materials is an ideal opportunity to build on what you know about your learners' lives and interests. For example, if you are choosing a reading text about a famous person, might it be someone your learners are particularly interested in?

8   **Ask a colleague to help you.** If you get into the habit of asking a colleague to look over drafts of your materials, you will get valuable ideas and suggestions. Mistakes are also far less likely to slip by two people! And if you offer to do the same for your colleague, you will get exposure to even more materials design ideas.

9   **Consider sharing your materials with colleagues.** The time involved in designing your own materials can really pay off when a group of colleagues are sharing materials around. Between you, you can build up a bank of materials for use with particular types of classes. These can be stored in a central area in the staff room. Knowing that others will use your materials is also an excellent incentive to make them as complete and clear as you can.

10   **Ask learners to contribute source texts.** Learners could be asked to search out texts which interest them on particular topics, and you could incorporate some of these into future materials. ESP (English for Special Purposes) learners especially may appreciate the chance for this sort of input – they, after all, know exactly what sort of texts they need to deal with.

11   **Ask learners for feedback on your materials.** They may be particularly willing to give this if they see it as an opportunity to influence the materials you and your colleagues will be designing for them in the near future. It can be very satisfying to learners to see their suggestions and views incorporated into materials.

Chapter 2   Meeting Learners' Needs

This chapter is essentially about people and processes. In the last chapter we talked a lot about the content of a language course – in this chapter we talk more about the people who are doing the learning. Our first set of suggestions looks at how classroom practice can best be adapted, so that the learning experience is inherently beneficial as well as simply efficient in language acquisition terms.

Students learn a great deal from each other. In small group situations, we can capitalize on this, and help them to derive the maximum benefit from each other. Our suggestions also point towards ways of avoiding some of the many things that can go wrong with inter-learner communication in small groups.

Teaching large groups of learners brings its own challenges. In the suggestions in this book, we concentrate on helping learners themselves to derive a good experience from those parts of their learning that they undertake in large groups.

Some classes are more demanding than others in terms of discipline. We offer some suggestions for keeping good order in your class, and encouraging learners to work with you to ensure a productive learning atmosphere for all.

We then look at the needs of some particular learner groups. We start by offering suggestions on how to meet the needs of mature learners. It is particularly important to adjust our approaches to mature learners in situations where the age range in a group may be quite broad, and where mature learners are learning alongside much younger learners. It is all too easy for the mature learners to feel uncomfortable or disadvantaged. We hope our suggestions will alert you to some ways around this.

We continue by offering some tips to help international students in particular. When learners study away from home, they often find themselves in a very different educational culture and climate, and may need some help to tune in to their new environment.

We end this chapter by offering some suggestions on ways that you can find out about the quality of your students' learning experiences. Feedback from learners can be really valuable, but it can also degenerate into routine ticked boxes on questionnaires and surface level decision making. We hope that our suggestions will help you to probe more deeply into your learners' experiences, and thereby will help you to continue to adjust and develop your own approaches.

6

Responding to learning needs in the classroom

A language classroom isn't just about helping learners to improve their language. It's also about trying to create a rich, supportive, memorable and life-enhancing learning experience. The following suggestions will help you to think about, and respond to, the needs of your students as social and learning human beings.

1   **Promote self-esteem.** Everyone is motivated by praise and encouragement. The more specific this can be, the better. For example, you could mention particular areas of improvement when giving feedback to individual learners. Personalized, detailed praise is likely to be most meaningful, since it is clearly the product of some thought. There is thus more of a chance that it will impact on learners' self-esteem.

2   **Provide cognitive challenge.** Well-chosen topics can help learners to learn far more than just language. Likewise, the tasks we ask them to do can engage more cognitive abilities than strictly language learning ones. For example, learners engaged in trying to work out a grammar 'rule' on the basis of examples are developing inferential skills as well as improving their language awareness.

3   **Provide a feeling of security.** Challenges are important, but they involve the risk of being wrong; and sometimes it's hard for learners to take this risk in public. Learners' requests for reliable rules may be one manifestation of this anxiety. Certain activities – controlled practice, 'rehearsals' in pairs or small groups – may help learners to feel safer. The use of interim rules, intended to evolve as learners' language develops, may also be reassuring.

4   **Allow personal expression.** Talking about ourselves seems to be a universal human need, and the language classroom is a very good place

to do it. The satisfaction of finding a code which expresses the learners' own meanings can make a piece of learning particularly memorable.

5   **Use your learners' areas of interest.** Interest is a good criterion for selecting topics and texts to study in class. If students are learning for a specific purpose, this is a vital part of making the class feel relevant for them; if they do not have identified future purposes in mind, then involving their different interests is still an opportunity for personalizing the class.

6   **Help them to develop links with native English speakers.** This could be via mail, e-mail, etc, as well as in person. Many learners would like to develop such links, but are unsure how to do it on their own. There is no better vindication of development as a language learner than to communicate successfully with native speakers!

7   **Bear in mind your learners' other educational experiences.** Adults may well have tried many approaches to language learning during their lives. Schoolchildren will be learning many subjects, no doubt also using varied approaches. All these experiences influence how they will feel about the approaches that you yourself want to take to language learning. Particularly if you are teaching outside your own country, you will need to think about how your ideas on language learning methodology fit with the local educational culture. You may have to strike a delicate balance, between respecting your learners' expectations and preferences, and introducing ideas that you think will work well.

8   **Share the rationale for what you are doing.** For example, if you use a lot of dictionary exercises because you think dictionary skills are an important part of becoming a good reader, say so. Revealing your own motivation is a way of asking your learners to cooperate with you and showing them that you trust them.

9   **Discuss learning strategies explicitly.** Explanations like the one referred to above are also important because they encourage learners to think about what sort of activities best help them to learn. Such awareness will help them in many situations, inside and outside the classroom.

10   **Involve learners in decision making where you can.** If learners can have input into the direction of a course or a lesson, they are likely to engage in it more deeply. Perhaps the ultimate goal here is to create an atmosphere where learners' suggestions can be heard, but where they still know that you, their teacher, are taking the long-term view and holding the course together.

7

Using pair and group work

Pair and group work have become almost synonymous with the modern, 'communicative' language classroom, and many teachers have found that these techniques have a lot to offer. Because they provide an opportunity for a genuine information and/or opinion exchange, they encourage very useful language practice. They also help learners to get used to working cooperatively and helping each other. The following tips should help you to use pair and group work thoughtfully and appropriately, and therefore effectively.

1 **Introduce the idea carefully.** Your learners may not be familiar with pair and group work. In this case it's important to discuss your reasons for using it (perhaps in L1), and to start using it little by little. After a pair or group activity ask your learners how they felt, and also give your own thoughts on how the activity contributed to the class's aims.

2 **Structure the work appropriately.** A class who are used to group and pair work, will be comfortable with a simple request to 'do this in pairs'. For a less experienced class, you yourself may need to organize the pairs, indicate who is to take which role, and give separate instructions for each stage of the activity. If you are doing pairwork in a class with an odd number of learners, you will need to make a group of three; consider modifying the task slightly for this group so that they can all participate.

3 **Make sure group members can have eye contact.** This will probably mean changing the seating arrangements so that members of the group are facing each other rather than facing the teacher. Even with fixed furniture, you can achieve eye contact by asking alternate rows of learners to turn round to face those sitting behind.

4 **Think about the task.** What do you think learners will gain by doing a particular task in pairs or groups? Don't assume that just because a coursebook suggests this way of working, that it is necessarily the best one. Some 'group' tasks can be made more effective in terms of information exchange and language use by adding an individual stage first, or by slightly differentiating what each group member is asked to do.

5   **Consider group size.** Different sizes may be best for different tasks. Larger groups give scope for more variety of roles and interaction patterns. Yet if all members are to have the chance to contribute productively, it can also be important to define roles clearly in advance.

6   **Make sure learners know what to do.** State the goal of the activity clearly and give staged instructions, where appropriate. If these are complicated, you could also write them on the board. Then ask a learner to explain the instructions in their own words, or – for a short activity – ask a pair to demonstrate for the class.

7   **Monitor group work discreetly.** Certainly don't interrupt groups: the whole idea is for the learners to operate as well as they can without you. Move around the class, quietly listening in; contribute to particular groups if they ask you to, or if you can see that they are stuck. Save your main feedback to give to the whole class after the group activity is finished.

8   **Stop the activity at the right moment.** This should be when most of the groups have completed or almost completed the task set, and before they start to get bored. For some tasks, it may be appropriate to set a time limit; for others, you need to go with the feel of the class. If any groups have been working slowly, warn them a couple of minutes in advance that you will have to stop shortly.

9   **Have something planned for early finishers.** This could be a continuation of the original task, or something quite different that emerges, such as study of a particular language point. If your learners are more independent, you could invite them to choose their own activity.

10 **Get pairs and groups to report to the class.** Many learners gain reassurance and emotional satisfaction from telling the whole class what work they did. It's also very valuable language practice: they get a 'second chance' to use the language of the task, in a situation where they will want to be as accurate as possible. You don't have to ask every group to report every time, as long as everyone gets a chance over a series of lessons.

11 **Be aware of L1 use.** If your class is monolingual, you may find that they sometimes use L1 during group work time. You need to be sensitive about this, because sometimes L1 serves a useful purpose – for example, learners may be conferring with each other on actually how to do the task. Try and make sure that they at least do the task itself in English.

8

Working with large classes

In many parts of the world, ESOL teachers find themselves working with groups of 60 or more learners. The following suggestions should help you to cope with the practical demands of large classes. They also explore ways of adapting techniques typically associated with smaller groups.

1   **Address learners by name whenever you can.** This helps learners to feel that you are aware of them as individuals and that their presence and contribution in class are important. We do not underestimate the difficulty of learning so many names; but techniques such as name cards, seating plans, or games at the start of the course can make the task more manageable.

2   **Don't compete for the floor.** If the level of background noise means that you cannot speak comfortably, stop speaking. Learners will almost always quieten down. This is a good way of demonstrating to them that they share the responsibility for creating a productive learning atmosphere.

3   **Elicit learners' practical help.** Management tasks like recording attendance, distributing and collecting materials and sharing around resources can be time consuming in a large class. Younger learners especially can enjoy taking on some of these responsibilities.

4   **Call on learners randomly, but equally.** During whole class work, it is you who must invite learners to speak and not everyone will get a chance in one lesson. Keep a simple record of who you have asked, so that others can be invited on future occasions. No learner should have to feel invisible!

5   **Use pair and group work.** Sometimes this feels chaotic in large classes, but it is the only way to give learners time to use the language for themselves. It is also an excellent opportunity for helping learners to start to develop independent learning skills, which will be particularly useful to them in a large class environment.

6   **Agree some alternative group configurations at the start of the course.** You may not want learners always to work with the same people, but a lot of time is saved when you ask them to form groups if they know who they are to go with. So having two or three pre-established group sets – according to the constraints of the particular classroom – is a good compromise.

7   **Monitor group work selectively.** During brief periods of group work you will not be able to monitor every group in detail. So give the bulk of your attention to just a small number of groups – and, again, make sure you rotate this fairly over a series of lessons.

8   **Agree a signal for quiet.** Noise levels during group work can seem high, and it may not be easy to get the class's attention again. A pre-arranged signal, such as clapping hands or ringing a bell, can bring the group back together. If you don't want to interrupt quite so brusquely, you could also try raising your arm as a request to 'finish off' – groups who finish then also raise their arms, until everyone has stopped.

9   **Take selective feedback on group activities.** Some of the groups who you were not able to monitor could be invited to report to the class on what they did. Try to make sure different group members get the chance to act as reporters.

10   **Invite the learners to write to you.** This does not necessarily mean at length, nor all the time, but at appropriate intervals, to give you feedback on their experience of the course. You can respond to the feedback orally, with the whole class or with an individual, if it seems necessary. The existence of a written communication channel can be reassuring for learners who have to 'share' the teacher with so many others during class time.

11   **Find out how colleagues cope with large classes.** There may be some institutional ground rules in operation that you can easily tap in to. For example, if the learners are already used to a certain signal for quiet or a certain approach to getting feedback on group activities, it will probably be easiest for you to do the same thing.

9

Keeping your class in good order

If you are working with small groups of motivated adults, who have powerful motives for learning English and who may be financing their own tuition, then you are unlikely to have to take *any* specific steps to 'keep order' in your classroom. But if you are working, for example, with children or teenagers who have not chosen to study English and are unsure of what benefits it might bring them, and/or if you are working with larger groups, then issues of classroom discipline are likely to be more salient for you. If learning is to take place in class, you need to maintain an ordered and productive atmosphere. The following suggestions should help you.

1   **Establish a code of conduct.** You need to make clear what your ground rules are about all aspects of classroom behaviour that are important to you. These might range from handing in homework on time to listening quietly when other learners are speaking. Depending on the nature of your class, you may discuss 'rules' explicitly or not – but more important than any discussion will be the way you put your code into practice over the first few lessons.

2   **Be sensitive to local and institutional culture**. Particularly if you are teaching in a foreign country, you need to find out what kinds of behaviour are generally considered appropriate in educational settings before trying to establish your own rules. Learners will expect you to have this understanding and to demonstrate it in your classes.

3   **Lead by example.** It is no use telling learners to arrive on time and then being late yourself, or demanding that they hand homework in on set days and then not returning it for weeks. Make sure that your own behaviour is guided by the same values that underpin the code of conduct that you are attempting to establish with your class.

4   **Be consistent in your reactions to inappropriate behaviour.** In many contexts, learners will continually try to test or stretch the code of conduct you have established, and you need to react consistently to this. For example, if you start off by expressing disapproval of late arrival, then continue to do so for as long as the behaviour persists – otherwise learners will think you have changed your mind.

5   **Carry out any threats you make.** If you say that you will not mark late homework, then don't mark it. That said, issues such as these in fact always involve a lot of judgement – there is bound to be a learner who has an excellent reason for handing in their work late. If the class or the particular learner are generally respectful of the code of conduct, then some flexibility may be appropriate – but if they are constantly pushing against the boundaries, you may need to be tough and run the risk of occasionally being unsympathetic to a genuine problem.

6   **Be fair.** It is essential to treat all learners equally, and not to have one rule for some and a different rule for others. Learners very soon pick up on this kind of favouritism and their respect for the teacher diminishes. It's natural to like some learners more than others, but it's important not to let this show.

7   **Talk to 'difficult' learners.** If a particular learner often causes problems in the class, then it's important to find out why. Make an arrangement to speak to them and ask, in a non-threatening way, what the problem is. Listen genuinely, but always move on to ask them what they can do about their behaviour. Sometimes, even the least cooperative learner can respond well to an approach that treats them like an adult and acknowledges that they may be having difficulties.

8   **Get the majority of the class on your side.** Even very 'difficult' classes usually contain just a few particularly disruptive individuals. If you can get the majority of the class to share your disapproval of the behaviour of such people, then the troublemakers will have little motivation to continue. One good technique is simply to stop the class until the disruption ceases. Most learners soon get bored with this and start to exert pressure on their disruptive classmates to behave.

9   **Talk to colleagues.** Compare notes with other teachers who teach your difficult classes, or who have done so in the past. They may be able to throw some light on what is going on, or give you some useful tips to improve things. Sometimes just to share experiences is useful, as it can help you to remember that you are not 'to blame' for a difficult situation that develops.

10   **Work with the institution.** If serious problems persist with a particular class or individual, then you should look to your institution for support. Exactly what can be done will vary considerably across institutions and cultures – but, one way or another, institutions have a final say about whether learners are allowed to attend, use facilities and graduate from one class to another. Institutional sanctions are, of course, a last resort, but you should remember that they are there if you need them.

10

Mature learners

It is important that we treat mature learners appropriately, and that they feel comfortable even when in groups or classes where they are working alongside much younger learners. The following suggestions may alert you to some of the principal issues which arise when working with mature learners, particularly when doing so in the context of courses that also include younger learners.

1   **Be aware of the anxieties that mature learners often have when first returning to studying.** They may have negative memories of their last experiences in education, and things may have changed a great deal since they were last students. Try not to allow them to feel vulnerable or exposed until they have had sufficient time to gain confidence.

2   **Remember that mature learners may know a lot!** They have probably studied English in a variety of situations and they may be particularly aware of what they are studying for now. It's worth giving them the chance to share their experience with the class. This can do a lot to increase their confidence in the group, especially in contexts where their younger counterparts are ahead of them in other ways, such as a familiarity with computers and electronic communication.

3   **Some mature learners tend to be demanding.** Such learners often take their studying a lot more seriously than some of their younger counterparts: one reason being that they are likely to have specific, often job-related, reasons for learning. They also tend to return to education with the more serious attitudes that may have been prevalent when they were last in an education system. Giving them an opportunity to discuss any worries about learning can be a major step to developing their confidence in their ability to succeed which, in turn, is probably one of the most significant factors predetermining their success.

4   **Remember that mature learners may be unfamiliar with contemporary approaches to language learning.** Similarly, mature learners may be out of practice in some academic skills, such as essay writing or notemaking. It is important to introduce them gently to 'new' approaches and help them to understand the rationale behind these. In some contexts, specifically designed study support, or learning skills induction programmes for mature learners can be most valuable to them, and much appreciated by them.

5   **Take care about your own assumptions.** Some mature learners will have covered ground you might never have expected them to have done, and others won't have experienced things you would have expected them to have covered. It's well worth spending a little time finding out a bit more about mature learners' views of their own strengths and weaknesses.

6   **Check out the needs and wants of your mature learners.** Ask them why they have chosen to study English, and how they believe it will fit into their future careers, or how it may feed into their plans for further studying.

7   **Treat mature learners appropriately!** They do not like being treated like children – but of course neither do younger learners, or children themselves! It is worth reminding yourself that at least some mature learners, who are just learners in your classroom, are likely to be experienced professionals like yourself in other places.

8   **Help mature learners to save face.** Mature people often don't like to be seen to get things wrong, especially when younger people are present. Watch out for occasions when feedback from assessments may raise this issue. Be sensitive to mature learners' feelings when they make contributions in class; if their comments or questions are shown to be 'silly' or inappropriate, such learners can take this as a serious blow to their confidence.

9   **Give mature learners the chance to interact well with the rest of the group.** When choosing groups for tasks or projects, it is often worth trying to get a good mix regarding age and background, to allow exchange of knowledge and experience in as many directions as possible.

10   **Be realistic about other demands on mature learners' time and energy.** They normally have abundant motivation and drive, but sometimes other pressures in their lives can affect the possibility of them meeting deadlines or targets.

11

Supporting learners away from home

If you are teaching in an English speaking country then many of your learners could be visitors from abroad, and may be joining your institution for a short period only. If you work in a dedicated language school, then the administrative and pastoral support systems of the institution should be geared up to this: if you work in another type of educational institution, your international students could be a minority group. In either case, the following suggestions should help you to assist your learners to make the most of their stay.

1 **Encourage your institution to arrange specialist induction provision for international students.** Pre-sessional meetings addressing aspects of cultural acclimatization, and looking at good study skills, can be of enormous benefit in helping international students get the most from their course.

2 **Produce clear information for your international students.** Try to ensure that they receive good documentation about their courses and about the institution and its environs, ideally before they arrive. International students are more likely to need to revisit such information again and again until they have tuned in to their new situation, and they can often do this more successfully when the information is in print rather than in easy-to-forget face-to-face formats.

3 **Help learners from other countries or cultures to understand what you will expect of them in assessments.** Assessment cultures vary widely around the world, and what is regarded as normal practice in some places is seen as cheating or plagiarism in others. It is important that all learners are aware of the ways they are expected to behave in preparing for and undertaking any kind of assessment. It can be particularly important to help learners adjust to those parts of their courses involving independent study, and about how to prepare for any assessment associated with such studies.

4   **Search for ways of lessening the isolation of international students.**
    Encourage them out of the institution, so they can absorb more of the
    local culture and make new contacts and friends. On the other hand, avoid
    putting them under any pressure to break their normal links with fellow
    learners from the same background.

5   **Be sensitive on issues of religion.** Some religions require followers to
    pray at specific times and in particular settings. This can be a problem for
    learners required to fit in with tight timetabling, and sensitive flexibility
    needs to be shown regarding their needs and rights.

6   **Help learners with special food requirements.** Learners visiting a foreign
    country may well be interested in trying out its food, but equally there
    could be limits on what they find acceptable. Gather feedback on
    appropriate alternatives that could be built into menus and catering
    provision. Advise those arranging catering at induction events to be
    especially sensitive about labelling food, so that international students
    don't become anxious about what they can and cannot eat.

7   **Consider getting past students from different countries to write an
    introductory guide to the idiosyncrasies of your country and institution!**
    This can be useful for new learners from abroad, and it's also good for
    staff and learners from the home country to see themselves through the
    eyes of people from other cultures. Any texts your learners produce can
    be a starting point for cross-cultural activities in lessons, and can help
    learners to find out about each others' backgrounds and feel that their
    own culture is valued.

8   **Recognize cultural differences regarding attitudes to alcohol.** Even if
    mainstream attitudes are alcohol tolerant, significant groups of learners
    come from cultures where alcohol may be forbidden on religious grounds.
    You should not expect groups of learners, whatever their background, to
    go on trips or visits which include a stop on the way back at a suitable
    pub! Class discussions of alcohol marketing strategies or pub social
    behaviours can be offensive or alien to learners whose culture forbids
    alcohol.

9   **Consider the special facilities needed by learners from other countries.**
    For example, toilet and washing facilities need to accommodate the
    different practices that are involved in some cultures or religions. When
    such learners attempt to make use of 'normal' facilities, their actions are
    in danger of being misunderstood.

10　**Consider the accommodation needs of learners from other cultures.**
Learners from some countries, when booking their place at your institution, may not know what is meant by, for example, 'hall of residence',
'single study bedroom' or 'shared student apartment'. Accommodation
literature needs to be written, or supplemented, so that all learners know
what each category of accommodation entails.

11　**Help learners from abroad to communicate with home, especially in
emergencies.** International telephone or fax charges are high, and learners
may not have access to locations where they can use such communications
in relative privacy. The costs, both financial and academic, of learners
having to make emergency visits home are serious, and ways need to be
found of helping learners to sort out some of the problems that could
lead them into such costs.

12

Designing feedback questionnaires

Questionnaires are widely used to collect feedback from learners on their experience in our institutions. You may be required to use an institutional questionnaire in any case. It is worth considering how you can gather feedback of your own by questionnaire, too. The following suggestions may give you some ideas to incorporate into your own feedback questionnaires.

1   **Keep the language level relatively simple and clear.** This way learners have a better chance of being sure what the question means. If you have a monolingual class and you speak their L1, give learners the option of using it in their responses. They will appreciate your efforts to help them to say what they really mean.

2   **Structured questionnaires can have the advantage of anonymity.** Even if using a mixed questionnaire containing open-ended questions as well, you may decide to issue the structured and open-ended parts separately because of this factor.

3   **Don't make questionnaires too long!** Learners – and anyone else involved – get bored if they have long questionnaires to complete, and the decisions or comments they make become 'surface' rather than considered ones. Although learners may be able to respond to a structured questionnaire of several pages in relatively few minutes, the fact that a questionnaire *looks* long can induce surface response behaviour.

4   **Consider the visual appearance of your questionnaires.** Go for a varied layout, with plenty of white space, so that it does not look like a solid list of questions. Use a mixture of response formats, such as deletions or selections from lists of options, yes/no choices, tick boxes, graduated scales, and so on – make it *look* interesting to complete.

5   **For every part of the questionnaire, have definite purposes, including positive ones.** Don't ask anything that could prove to be superfluous or of passing interest only. Ask about positive experiences as well as searching for weaknesses.

6   **Plan your evaluation report before you design your feedback questionnaire.** It helps a great deal if you know exactly how you plan to collate and use the responses you will get from your questionnaires. Working out the things you hope to include in your report often alerts you to additional questions you may need to include, and (particularly) to superfluous questions that would not actually generate any information of practical use to you.

7   **Make each question simple and unambiguous.** If learners' interpretations of the questions vary, the results of a survey are not valid enough to warrant statistical analysis of any sort. In particular, it's worth ensuring that in structured questions, learners are only required to make decisions involving a single factor.

8   **Ask yourself 'what does this question really mean?'** Sometimes, your reply to yourself will contain wording which will work better in your questionnaire than the original idea you started with. When designing your questions, ask some of your learners 'what do *you* think this really means?'

9   **Avoid safe middle ground in scales.** For example, the scale 'strongly agree, agree, undecided, disagree, strongly disagree' may give better results if the 'undecided' option is omitted, forcing respondents to make a decision one way or the other (or to *write* 'can't tell' on the questionnaire, which then has the validity of a conscious decision).

10 **Be aware that some respondents will make the choices they believe they are expected to make.** Respondents from some cultures set out to 'please' the person gathering the feedback, perhaps thinking of possible recriminations if critical comments are traced back to their authors.

11 **Keep prioritizing questions short and simple.** For example, if learners are asked to rank seven factors in order of value (or importance), it may be easy enough to analyze the best and worst choices, but difficult to make a meaningful analysis of 'middle ground'.

12 **Pilot your draft questionnaire.** There is no better way to improve a structured questionnaire than to find out what learners actually do with it!

13   **Feed back the results to your respondents.** Tell them about the changes that are proposed on the basis of the results from the questionnaire. Otherwise people are likely to become disillusioned about the whole process of giving feedback.

14   **Remember that learners' responses can be influenced by their mood at the moment of answering the question.** Ideally, you may wish to balance this source of variation out in one way or another; for example, by issuing a similar questionnaire at another time, and comparing responses, or by including some alternative questions in other parts of your questionnaire which 'test' the same agenda so you can be alerted to inconsistency in responses due to swings of mood.

15   **Don't leave big spaces for learners to fill in their replies to open-ended questions.** You can compensate for this restriction later with 'any other comments?' space. If learners responses are necessarily short, you are more likely to get easily interpreted answers to your questions, which helps make analysis more fruitful.

16   **Try to achieve a good response rate.** When questionnaires are filled in during contact time, you are more likely to get everyone's views. If questionnaires are taken away by learners to be sent back later, there is a tendency to get lower response rates, and the learners who actually go to the trouble of responding may not be representative of the whole group.

17   **Give learners some free ranging questions.** For example, it's worth asking them 'What other questions should be included in future editions of this questionnaire?', and inviting them to supply their own answers to the questions they think of. Such data is unsuitable for any statistical purposes, but is valuable in qualitative analysis of feedback from learners, and can often touch on aspects that relate to potential quality enhancement developments.

18   **Don't accumulate piles of uninterpreted questionnaire data!** It's best to make a deliberate effort to produce a summary report (even if only for your own private use) for each set of data. A pile of feedback responses quickly becomes out of date as new developments are implemented in courses. Also, it is worth helping learners to see that it is worth their while to provide feedback data, and showing them that you take the data seriously enough to analyse it straightaway.

Chapter 3   Language Work in the Classroom

This is the most substantial chapter of our book, and also the chapter that looks most closely at specific techniques for teaching various aspects of language. We offer a range of suggestions on how you can choose to go about teaching vocabulary, pronunciation, listening, reading, speaking, writing and grammar. In practice, of course, you will often be doing many of these at the same time, so perhaps this chapter should be viewed as a whole rather than as separate agendas.

We also look at various resources you can use to support your teaching: your coursebook, and also various sources not originally produced for language learning. We end the chapter with some suggestions about how you can use games, role plays and that most commonly available resource in the developed world, 'the news', to help your learners to develop their command of English, and their confidence in using English.

13

Teaching vocabulary

A great deal of the meaning of language resides in the meanings associated with individual words and phrases. By learning a few basic words and set phrases, a beginner can get some meanings across. Language learning syllabuses almost always specify vocabulary items or areas for learners to concentrate on. The following suggestions should enable you to help your learners to work effectively with the vocabulary of their target language.

1 **Distinguish receptive and productive vocabulary needs.** Some learners, who intend to read extensively in English, may need to recognize a lot of words that they may never have to use themselves. Others, for example, general English beginners, are probably hoping that the words they learn will be available for both recognition and use. Try and tailor your teaching to these different needs.

2 **Consider teaching new vocabulary in related sets.** You could choose sets of hyponyms (eg, names of family relations), or sets that are linked to the same context (eg, subjects studied at school). Most people find it easier to learn lots of new words if they are presented in a related set. If you are teaching a set of nouns, you can include some verbs which are typically used with them (eg, *study* English/maths/geography at school, *take* an exam).

3 **Vary your explanation techniques.** There are many possibilities for clarifying the meaning of words that your learners don't know: definitions, examples, visuals, mimes – to name but a few. If you use varied techniques, you show your learners that there are many ways of understanding and remembering a word.

4 **Teach the grammar of vocabulary items.** This idea refers to the word itself, or to the word in a phrase. For example, in the case of a verb, does it have an irregular past? In the case of an adjective, is it usually followed by a certain preposition? Some of this information may be available in the text where your learners meet the word, and you can give extra

information yourself. Understanding how a word 'works' is an important part of knowing that word.

5   **Encourage awareness of collocations.** Even when teaching basic vocabulary, you can show how words often combine in certain ways. For example, Spanish learners studying colours would be interested to note that English says 'black and white', whereas Spanish says 'blanco y negro'. Set phrases, such as 'hard work', can also be particularly useful to point out.

6   **Spend some time on connotative meaning.** You can turn connotation into a window on the target culture. Take a simple item like 'train'. For many British speakers, this item has the connotation of a fast and frequent, though also expensive and unreliable, mode of transport. The item probably would not have these connotations for someone from a country without a developed railway system.

7   **Help learners to be aware of register.** Is the target vocabulary item usually associated with either written or spoken language? Is it formal, informal, literary, technical, slang? What clues does the context of the word give about its register?

8   **Look at word formation.** An understanding of common prefixes and suffixes, for example, can open up the meaning of many words. How much conscious emphasis you place on this will probably depend on the learners' first language. Speakers of Latin languages will understand many English morphemes immediately; speakers of languages less close to English will need to spend more time on these aspects.

9   **Use direct translation carefully.** Learners often request translations, and if you can give them this it is an efficient way of explaining a word. But it's also worth drawing attention to the ways in which words are not equivalent. Perhaps the 'translations' differ in terms of connotation, register, grammar, collocation? You can use dictionary study activities to emphasize this point.

10 **Teach conscious vocabulary learning strategies.** This is one of the areas of study where it is particularly beneficial for learners to apply their own 'techniques'; to remember items or work out the meaning of new ones. It's especially useful for you to show them strategies that they can use outside class. For example, they might: keep a vocabulary notebook; classify new words they have seen; revise new vocabulary at intervals. Your role can be to explore various techniques with the class, and help each learner to find out which ones suit them best.

14

Teaching pronunciation

Pronunciation is an area of language use where it is particularly difficult to exert conscious control. And yet, it's important. For beginners, or for those who have learnt mainly from written texts, poor pronunciation can be a obstacle to being understood. For more advanced learners, pronunciation can still be an issue; inappropriate intonation may mean that they 'give the wrong message' when they speak. The importance of pronunciation work is being increasingly recognized in coursebooks, and you may well find yourself using a book that contains specific pronunciation activities. The following suggestions, then, should help you to make the most of explicit pronunciation work with your learners.

1   **Learn how to describe pronunciation.** Familiarize yourself with the phonemic symbols for English, and with a system for describing some basic intonation patterns. These are challenging tasks, but they can bring rich dividends. The knowledge will help you to understand more clearly what your learners are aiming for in terms of pronunciation, and what their problems are.

2   **Record your learners' speech.** It is best to choose moments where one learner at a time is speaking. Listen to the recordings and see where their main difficulties lie; especially if you have a monolingual class, they will probably have difficulties in common. You can then think about which of their difficulties are most significant: which are likely to form a barrier to effective communication?

3   **Be aware of your own pronunciation.** Whether or not you are a native speaker of English, your accent is probably different from the Received Pronunciation which your learners may regard as 'correct'. Learners can have strong views about some accents being superior to others! Talk to them about different accents, emphasizing that there is more than one acceptable model.

4   **Teach pronunciation a little at a time.** Pronunciation will improve naturally if you ensure that your learners do lots of listening and speaking. Intensive pronunciation work can help, but short, fairly frequent sessions are the most useful.

5   **Teach some phonemic symbols.** This can be done gradually, so as not to overload learners. Once they know the symbols, you have a very useful metalanguage available for talking about pronunciation.

6   **Work on learners' perception of target sounds.** Awareness of a sound is the first step to being able to produce it. But if a sound does not exist in your learners' first language, or is not significant for meaning, then they may find it very difficult to hear the essential characteristics of the English sound. 'Minimal pair' exercises can be useful here.

7   **Tell learners how target sounds are physically articulated.** Especially if learners are having trouble with a sound, an explicit description of the voice, place and manner of articulation can be useful. You can use a diagram of the mouth, such as appears in many pronunciation books, to help you here.

8   **Work on learners' perception of intonation.** English intonation is, of course, very significant for meaning. It especially has to do with the 'shared knowledge' of speakers involved in a conversation: whether speakers perceive what they are saying as new information, or as already understood. To demonstrate this idea, you will probably need to use recordings involving several turns of dialogue, where there is a context to help learners to see how 'shared knowledge' is built up and assumed.

9   **Get learners to produce whole utterances, and combinations of utterances, during pronunciation practice.** That way they work in tandem on intonation and on the correct pronunciation of individual sounds in context. The sounds which make up words can change and, in some cases, even disappear, according to the context of pronunciation, and these changes are intimately linked to the rhythm of the utterance.

10 **Let learners listen to recordings of themselves.** This can be a valuable awareness raising strategy; they may well hear features of their pronunciation that they simply do not have time to notice when actually speaking. As a result, they may be able to work on weak areas consciously.

15

Teaching listening

Processing language in real time brings special demands for language learners. Unable to look at the language again, or to use aids such as dictionaries, they can become completely lost in a text that they would probably follow if it was presented in written form. Listening work in the classroom is intended to give learners practice at understanding spoken language, and also to help to develop strategies to make up for what they do not manage to understand. The following suggestions should help you to make the most of listening activities.

1   **Give as much exposure as you can.** Particularly exposure to spontaneous spoken speech, because this is what your learners will hear most of in an English speaking environment. You can provide a lot of this exposure yourself by the way you talk in class. Find a moment to tell a story or an anecdote, or to describe something without choosing your words too carefully. This slightly more 'social' talk, perhaps outside the main structure of the lesson, can approximate more closely to the non-classroom speech learners are aiming to understand.

2   **Do your classroom management in English.** This provides another opportunity for your learners to hear semi-planned or sometimes spontaneous speech. They will be well-motivated to listen to what you say, and the context of the classroom will make understanding easier. Learners often get a lot of satisfaction from the idea that the class conducts its business in English, and that they can understand and participate in this.

3   **Use audio and video recordings.** These bring essential variety to the class, and considerably enrich the exposure that is possible. Give your learners practice at getting the basic meaning of a text with just one hearing – this, after all, is the situation they will face outside. Hearing a recording through also gives them a chance to listen without doing anything else, which can make a pleasant change.

4   **Provide a context for any recording you use.** A context makes listening and understanding much easier; learners will know what sort of thing to expect. It also approximates better to listening outside; in everyday life, we rarely listen to anything 'cold', without any idea of what it will be about.

5   **Give learners a reason for listening.** Before you play the recording you can give learners a task based on what they will hear, or even some questions to answer. This can help learners to focus on key information and filter out 'noise'. Especially for lower level learners who find understanding speech difficult, it is very motivating to successfully complete a task from spoken input.

6   **Use listening for pleasure, too.** You can also use radio stories, films, etc, where the motivation for listening lies in the interest of the text itself. This is something that learners can do outside class, too – and they are more likely to do so if they build up confidence by doing it in class first.

7   **Show learners they don't have to understand every word.** Activities like listening for gist, listening for specific information or listening to confirm predictions can wean learners away from trying to follow every word. This type of activity is easiest with texts that are not too dense, and which include features like hesitation, repetition and redundancy, which we associate with real time communication in the world outside the classroom.

8   **Let learners experience a variety of accents and dialects.** You will probably want to do most of your listening work with the accent(s) your learners are most likely to experience. But it is helpful to sensitize them to the existence of a wider range of accents, and to the fact that an unfamiliar accent is more difficult to understand.

9   **Find out what your learners need to listen to.** If they are aiming to listen to relatively formalized speech events such as lectures or sales presentations then you could show them some of the typical characteristics of their target genre. For example, does it usually follow a certain order? Can you isolate key language that the speaker might use to show they are moving from one phase to the next?

10   **Teach learners the strategies needed to control the input they get.** In a face-to-face situation, the 'listener' is very active, indicating how well they are following the speaker. Perhaps using some transcripts of spontaneous speech, show your learners how they can indicate that they are understanding, or how they can ask for repetition or clarification. Having

such strategies at their disposal can give learners confidence to interact with more competent speakers outside the classroom. By doing this, they get themselves more exposure and so have more learning and practice opportunities.

11 **Consider setting listening tasks for homework.** If you are working in a well-resourced context, where your institution has plenty of tapes to lend and your learners have tape players at home, you can set them listening tasks to do outside the class. This gives them exposure to far more spoken input than they could get if all your listening tasks were confined to the classroom.

16

Teaching reading

Reading is both a matter of quality and of quantity. Students need to learn the skills of target language reading, and they also need exposure to a rich variety of written texts. Such exposure will contribute to general language improvement as well as fostering reading competence itself. The following suggestions should help you to effectively select and exploit texts, and encourage good reading habits in your learners.

1   **Supplement the readings in your textbook.** Extra readings are usually easy to get hold of, and are an opportunity for you to both respond to your learners' particular interests and to bring new ideas into the class. You can also ask learners to bring in texts for use in class. In these ways, you can give your learners exposure to a wider variety of texts than they might otherwise get.

2   **Use a good proportion of 'authentic' texts.** Successful reading of texts from the world outside the classroom is very motivating, and exposure to such sources can provide language development opportunities on conscious and unconscious levels. Adjust the task associated with the reading to make the text accessible. See 22, Exploiting authentic written texts.

3   **Build up a context.** You may work with texts where understanding is particularly dependent on a knowledge of the context in and for which they were produced. (Newspaper articles are an obvious example.) Help learners to access the background that the text does not supply. If you choose to work with short extracts of texts, you will also need to give your learners the background information that the 'full' text supplies.

4   **Give learners a reason for reading.** A task appropriate to the text can encourage suitable reading strategies and may give practice in some longer-term reading goals. Tasks which learners recognize as relevant to their reasons for studying English are, of course, particularly motivating.

5   **Use questions carefully.** The technique of having learners answer a series of comprehension questions on a reading is well known. If you use it, try to go beyond surface comprehension to involve learners in the ideas behind the text: for example, you could ask about the author's main message, position or attitude.

6   **Use reading as an input to other tasks.** Reading as a means to specific ends is very common in the world outside the classroom, and many learners may need to exploit English language texts in this way. For example, the task of writing a summary of two or three textbook passages would mirror one of the ways that EAP learners need to read.

7   **Talk about good reading habits.** Especially in the earlier stages, you will need to design activities that explicitly target useful reading behaviour like using titles and illustrations, skimming over unknown words or working out meaning from context. You can also get learners to think about ways in which they read effectively in L1. By talking about good reading strategies, you give learners the option of attempting to use them consciously.

8   **Talk about text structure.** If you are working with many examples of a particular type of text, you may find that their organization has things in common. For example, is the same section of the text the one which carries the most important information? Do the texts open and close in routine ways? (For example, letters.) Insights into text structure can make reading much easier.

9   **Teach dictionary skills.** This means not only when to use a dictionary, but how: practice in looking up words, and in understanding the information and examples, will give learners confidence to read outside class. Many learners start off by using a bilingual dictionary; this can indeed be useful, but a good monolingual one is even more so. By studying its explanations and examples, learners can gain a richer picture of the meanings of words they do not know.

10 **Encourage reading for pleasure.** Include this as a class activity occasionally, with short texts. Then help learners to choose suitable books, magazines, etc, from the school library or self-access centre and ask them sometimes about their reading. Find out what they like to read in their first language, and see if you can guide them to accessible L2 equivalents.

17

Teaching speaking

In many ways you can't teach speaking. In real time, spontaneous oral production, there is little chance for conscious reflection – learners must rely on what has already become automatic for them. In class, your most important role is to provide practice opportunities for speaking. The following tips should help you to see how.

1   **Run the class in English.** The more English your learners can use in class, the better. If English is the language of classroom management, they will need to speak it to get things done. That said, a monolingual group will inevitably prefer to use L1 at times and you need to be sensitive about this. L1 use can also have an important social function for your group: to gain an insight into this, try to notice the circumstances in which they tend to use it.

2   **Use plenty of group and pair work.** For obvious reasons, this maximizes the class time available for learners to speak. Each format has its own advantages: a pair puts pressure on both parties to contribute, whereas a group gives practice in negotiating more complex interaction patterns. See 7, Using pair and group work.

3   **Make activities as spontaneous as possible.** Most talk in the world outside the classroom is unplanned, and learners need to practise this kind of speaking. Be accepting of the idea that their talk in such situations will inevitably be less accurate than in a more structured task.

4   **Use guided activities where necessary.** That sounds like a contradiction with tip 3, but really it's a question of sensitivity to starting points. Learners with little experience of oral work may clam up completely if given a task involving spontaneous speech. For such learners, the scaffolding of a learnt or heavily guided dialogue can give much needed confidence.

5   **Consider role plays.** They have been criticized on the grounds that they ask learners to make believe – but they also provide an opportunity for learners to imagine a wide variety of situations, relationships and attitudes and attempt to convey these in language. If you use role plays regularly, learners can 'catch on' and willingly suspend their disbelief. For more ideas on role plays, see 26.

6   **Use task-based activities.** A good way to generate language without putting learners into roles is to ask them to collaborate towards an objective, for example, to list the qualities of a good teacher. Language is then a means to an end as well as a subject of practice. Tasks like this can feel very realistic to learners.

7   **Try out new tasks with friends or colleagues.** Sometimes it's hard to tell what kind of language a particular speaking task is likely to generate. If you do the task yourself, or ask some other competent speakers to do it, you will get a better idea of its linguistic demands.

8   **Make learners aware of varied speaking needs.** Many learners associate speaking with free discussion, where fluency is more important than accuracy; they may not expect other kinds of speaking activity. In the world outside, though, they may need to use planned, or semi-planned, as well as spontaneous speech.

9   **Give some practice at long turns.** The skill of telling a story, or giving a short presentation, is very different from the skill of participating in a conversation or oral transaction. Practise this, especially if you know your learners need to perform a particular type of long turn. It's often useful to pay special attention to linking words and phrases, which can make a long turn sound smooth.

10   **Link speaking to other tasks.** In this way different kinds of speech can be practised. For example, if groups of learners are preparing a guide to their town, they will need to speak to brainstorm ideas, to manage the production of the written version and to assess its acceptability: three very different types of speech.

11   **Correct spoken language selectively.** The point of speaking activities is for learners to produce language in real time – do not inhibit them by picking up on every mistake. One technique is to go around listening to groups, and keep some time in the lesson to discuss 'common' mistakes. Not all learners' language use will change as a result, but some may be ready to make the change you are asking for.

12   **Create an atmosphere of acceptance.** Many learners find it rather threatening to speak in the target language. You can help them get over their fear by always responding with respect to what they say, and encouraging other class members to do the same. Respond to the content of what they say, before deciding whether to correct any inaccuracies.

18

Teaching writing

Extended writing is a skill in itself, one which many learners will need in target situations. It also provides opportunities for creativity and self-expression, which many learners appreciate. And it is, of course, an important part of overall language learning – it provides opportunities for conscious reflection that can play an important role in consolidating recent learning.

1   **Ask learners to produce a variety of text types.** Basic styles of writing such as narrative, static description, process description, argument, etc, demand different language skills: the styles are brought to life in different tasks and text types. Involve learners in as many of these as are appropriate to their level and reasons for learning.

2   **Analyse particularly important text types yourself.** If you know that your learners need to produce, for example, reports of laboratory experiments, then get hold of some examples of such reports and see if you can discover any typical patterns of language use and structure. Share these insights with your learners.

3   **Combine writing with other tasks.** Asking learners to respond in writing to something they have read or heard gives a reason for writing and clearly specifies an audience. These are two important characteristics of writing in the world outside the classroom.

4   **Don't always leave writing for homework.** Writing in groups, or checking and editing each other's drafts, are valuable learning activities and a good use of class time. This type of activity may also be an opportunity for learners to write to a real audience: to peers, to school authorities, to a local newspaper, etc.

5   **Encourage multiple drafts and revisions.** It's simply not realistic to ask learners to go from a blank page to a final product in one go! Drafts are an opportunity to write without inhibitions, and learners themselves, their peers and teachers, all have a potential role in providing feedback to be incorporated into revisions.

6   **Give examples of multiple drafts.** Learners can sometimes think that rewriting is just a matter of incorporating corrections and producing a clean copy. Help them to see that drafts are a useful way of developing content, too.

7   **Accept that there will be many mistakes in early drafts.** This is particularly the case for less proficient learners, of course. Help learners to see texts with lots of mistakes as a natural stage. Try to build up an atmosphere where peer as well as teacher feedback is seen as useful on the way to a final product.

8   **Emphasize quality in the final product.** In the world outside the classroom, demands on written products are high: we expect an appropriate range of vocabulary and sentence patterns, as well as accuracy. Learners need experience of getting to this final, polished stage where work is considered ready for formal public scrutiny.

9   **Give feedback on content as well as on form.** When learners engage with a task, their main motivation for writing is to convey a message – they may have put a lot of thought into the content of their writing. Respond to their writing as communication first, and language practice second.

10 **Be selective when correcting mistakes.** Learners like to be corrected, but will be demotivated by seeing a page of their work covered in red. Neither will they be able to learn from such extensive feedback. Concentrate on the most basic errors, those that impede communication and those that you think learners are most ready to learn about.

11 **Agree a key for correction.** Especially with more advanced learners, you can use codes like t (tense), w.o. (word order), or v (vocabulary) to indicate the place and nature of an error, while still giving learners the chance to correct the word themselves. When learners get the work back they can attempt to make their own corrections. Sometimes they will do this easily, at other times they may need to ask you and/or a classmate what the problem actually is. In either case, the process of self-correction draws attention to the error and helps to make the correction memorable. All of this helps learning.

12 **Look back during the course.** At appropriate moments, encourage learners to look critically at earlier writing tasks, and perhaps work on something similar again. They will be motivated by seeing how much they have improved, and may be reminded of important bits of learning.

19

Teaching grammar

There has been much debate about explicit grammar teaching – arguments about whether it does any good, or about what approach might be most effective. Yet it remains a valuable mainstay of many language courses, and institutional context is a major influence on the policies adopted by individual teachers. Learners also usually expect to concentrate on grammar at some point during a course. The following tips are options for you to consider and adapt where necessary.

1   **Expect grammatical errors.** They are a normal part of language development and you can't get rid of them by pointing them out. Learners might produce a new form correctly in a controlled practice activity, but get it wrong again the next day – this is normal, too. With lots of opportunities to use language for meaning, and focus on accuracy at appropriate points, they will improve over time.

2   **Provide learners with opportunities to use their full grammatical range.** This means providing meaning-focused production activities, where learners can choose what language they produce within the role play, task, etc. You may choose an activity which creates an opportunity to use recently studied grammatical forms, for the benefit of learners who are ready to consolidate in this way.

3   **Consider explicit practice activities.** These are activities where language is more controlled – the prime purpose of the activity is to practise a recently studied form. Such activities usually have a meaning-focused dimension, but learners are told what language they should use to express the meaning. For example, learners might be invited to discuss weekend plans using the 'going to' future. These kinds of activities can be especially beneficial for less confident learners, and for those whose previous learning has been highly form-focused.

4   **Correct errors carefully.** In both meaning-focused and form-focused activities, errors will persist. As always, your attitude to correction and feedback should depend on the purpose of the activity and on what you think your learners are ready to learn.

5   **Make grammar presentations meaningful.** You may choose to present explicitly a new grammatical form; certainly, this is a widely used technique. If you do, make sure your presentation highlights the meaning dimension – elements of the semantic significance of the target form. You can check whether learners have understood this by using 'concept' questions, which highlight an aspect of the situation which makes the meaning of the target form clear.

6   **Use discovery techniques.** An alternative to grammatical presentation is to show learners examples of a grammatical form in various contexts and to encourage them to work out its significance. The contexts can be drawn from both 'authentic' and 'non authentic' sources. Many modern textbooks use a combination of discovery and presentation techniques; experience will help you find the right balance for your learners.

7   **Give clear and simple explanations.** At times you will be called upon to summarize the correct use of a grammatical form. Research your explanation, ideally in more than one grammar book – and then give an explanation that you feel best meets the current stage of your learners' language awareness. Show them that explanations are really just workable simplifications; exceptions to 'rules' will inevitably be found. They are an opportunity to refine one's understanding of the rule in question.

8   **Capitalize on learners' existing knowledge.** Especially if they have previously learnt in a formal way, your learners will no doubt possess a grammatical metalanguage which you can tap into. Find out how they express the 'rules' that they already know, and work from there. Even if the rules they know are incomplete, they are probably still useful for the learners; so if you find you need to contradict them, do so sensitively.

9   **Balance the conditions for grammar improvement.** Meaning-focused work, restricted practice, explanation and analysis all have a part to play in building up the grammatical knowledge that learners have spontaneously available. Different conditions will help different learners at different times. So the important thing is to ensure that lessons or series of lessons contain a good balance.

10   **Keep on providing rich exposure.** Even in a grammatically focused course it's important for learners to read and listen to texts where complexity goes beyond the structures they have learnt about. Modify tasks to make texts like this accessible. Subconsciously learners will start to get used to the unfamiliar structures, and will be more receptive if the structures are focused on again at a later point.

20

Making good use of your coursebook

Very many of the English language courses being taught around the world are based on coursebooks. The coursebook may have been chosen by the teacher(s), or imposed from above; however it was chosen, it often becomes the linchpin of the course. The suggestions that follow should help you to use your coursebook creatively: to make the most of what it offers, without allowing it to restrict you and your learners.

1   **Use the coursebook as a management aid.** The predictable shape of its units offers a structure for your lessons and reassures learners, especially in the early stages of the course. Once the structure is established, it can become a platform for experimentation. Innovation is easier when everyone is starting from the same place.

2   **Be selective.** No matter how appropriate a coursebook for your programme, it is unlikely that all the activities, in the precise order presented, will be right for your learners. Within the broad structure of the book, decide what to use and what to leave out, replace, or come back to another time.

3   **Use coursebooks as resource books.** Many modern coursebooks include free standing activities, or coherent series of activities such as a story in episodes. Often they also include a grammar section, verb tables and a chart of phonemic symbols. If you need supplementary material for your main coursebook, then another coursebook could be a very good place to look!

4   **Adapt activities, where appropriate.** You might see an activity as being broadly beneficial, and yet unsuitable from a particular perspective: perhaps the cultural content is inappropriate, or the skills emphasis not

what you want at that moment. By adapting the activity to your particular learners, you offer them more opportunities to engage with it and gain benefit from it.

5   **Build in learners' real experience whenever you can.** Use the activities in the coursebook as an opportunity for learners to talk about their own lives, experiences and opinions. The more chances they have in class to say what they want to in the way they want to say it, the more likely it is that they will be able to use their classroom learning in the world outside.

6   **Help learners to understand the rationale of the coursebook.** If you talk to your learners about the reasoning behind the activities they are doing and the way the coursebook is structured, you offer them more resources for learning. They can use their awareness of coursebook's intentions to develop more conscious strategies for learning, both in class and outside. They can also talk to you about their own preferred ways of learning.

7   **Show learners some differences between coursebook language and the language of the outside world.** Spoken language in coursebooks is rarely 'authentic', and there can be good reasons for this. But more advanced learners especially may benefit from looking analytically at the difference between a made up or edited dialogue in a coursebook and an unscripted dialogue produced by native speakers. If you can, record some unscripted spoken language as an occasional supplement to your coursebook. See 21, Collecting natural language data.

8   **Use problem areas as a springboard for discussion.** There may be elements of your coursebook that you are unhappy with. These may be rather insidious: for example, does the coursebook seem to imply a negative attitude to particular social groups? If you find difficulties like this, then you can discuss them with your learners. Once negative stereotypes or other inappropriate attitudes are out in the open, their power is considerably diminished.

9   **Use the coursebook as a basis for negotiation with learners.** A significant advantage of a coursebook is that it allows learners, as well as the teacher, to see what is planned for the course. As learners become more aware of the purpose of various elements of the book, and of how they themselves prefer to learn, then they may be prepared to share with you some of the responsibility for deciding what happens in lessons. In this case, groups of learners or individuals can select from the book those activities that they feel are most appropriate to them.

10   **Use the coursebook for your own development.** A good coursebook will not only enhance your knowledge of how English works, it will also offer you space in which to grow as a teacher. As you use the book, you can reflect consciously on how well its different aspects are working for you, and why. You can ask other teachers how they handle the book, and maybe observe them. You can ask a colleague to observe you, and then talk together about what happens. The most important thing is attitude: see the book as a learning opportunity.

21

Collecting natural language data

Coursebooks and other teaching resources give teachers plenty of language data to work with, but at times you may prefer to work with written or spoken texts you have collected yourself. If you have a specific purposes class, you might want to collect data that is directly relevant to their language needs. If you have a more general class, you might want to vary their language exposure. The following suggestions should help you to collect usable natural language data. Most of them concentrate on spoken data, since that is the most difficult to collect!

1   **Obtain permission.** If you are recording people's speech, or taking documents relating to an organization, you need to ask for permission. Even for published or broadcast material, which is in the public domain, you should make sure you are not breaking copyright by using it for teaching.

2   **Be realistic about what you can record.** Unless you have excellent equipment and much skill, it will be difficult to obtain a coherent recording of more than two or three speakers at once. Background noise may also be a problem, depending on where you are recording. So don't be too ambitious, and plan for plenty of trial runs.

3   **Choose the best medium for recording.** A decision whether to use audio or video may be dictated entirely by practical considerations. If you have access to both, think about their respective advantages and disadvantages. Video captures paralinguistic features such as gestures, but it is more obtrusive and the sound quality may not be as good as that of an audio recording. Unless you are particularly experienced, it is also far more complicated and difficult to set up and actually use.

4   **Choose the situations carefully.** If you have a specific purposes class, can you get direct access to any of your learners' target situations? Or can you interview specialists in the areas they are interested in? For a general class, are there situations you would like to cover but which are absent from your learners' usual materials?

5   **Record short texts where possible.** Two minutes of speech will give you about 400 words of text, and contain plenty of interesting features you can look at with your learners. It is often easier for learners to deal with natural language data in relatively short chunks. For example, you can record interviews in two or three parts, or record a situation and then an observer's summary of it.

6   **Observe the situation you record and make notes about it as soon as you can.** Many important aspects of a situation are lost in a recording. Even if your learners will work from the recording alone, you still need notes to maximize your own understanding of what went on. Your observation notes can also be the basis for a written introduction to the spoken text your learners are to work with.

7   **Observe other similar situations.** This can give you an idea of the typicality of your data and also help you to understand it better. For example, if you record a tutorial in a particular institution, observing other tutorials will give you a more informed perspective on the language you have recorded.

8   **Talk to insiders about your data.** This tip particularly applies if you are working with language with which you yourself are unfamiliar: for example, a specialized technical presentation or written report. Subject specialists can help you to understand the communicative purposes which underlie the language, and perhaps suggest other related situations that you could record.

9   **Consider setting up a situation.** If you want more general examples of spontaneous spoken interaction, you can obtain these by putting speakers together and asking them to carry out a task; for example, ask about each other's families, remember and then report back. Some well-known modern coursebooks use exactly this technique. It's a good way of getting spontaneous data under fairly controlled conditions. You could also ask speakers to carry out some of the tasks in your learners' coursebook; learners may be very interested to compare their performance with that of the speakers you record.

10   **Consider using broadcast sources.** There are some situations that you will never be able to record, for reasons of practicality and confidentiality: doctor–patient interviews for example. TV or film dramatizations of these events do have at least some language features in common with the 'real thing', and could be exploited in teaching. You will, of course, need to check copyright regulations before using broadcast material in teaching.

11   **Transcribe your recording.** You will probably find this quite difficult the first time you do it, and you will need to listen to the recording several times. But it's an essential step if you are going to exploit the data you have collected. Try and get down all the words of each speaker, including hesitations, false starts, ums and ahs, etc.

22

Exploiting authentic written texts

The term 'authentic' can, of course, be controversial. Here we use it in its simplest sense, to refer to texts originally produced for a purpose other than language learning. Many teachers choose to work with such texts; they can help to give learners a general wide exposure, or they may be needed as a response to specifically identified language needs. The following suggestions should help you to gain maximum pedagogic benefit from the authentic written texts you use.

1   **Work with meaning first.** Before looking at the language of a text in detail, it's best to ask learners to work with it as a piece of communication. There are a wide variety of tasks you can use to create an enjoyable learning activity and/or a simulation of likely text to use outside the classroom. You can go on to look at detailed language in the same lesson, and you can also save up texts learners have worked with for later language study.

2   **Grade the task to suit your learners' level.** The most accessible tasks are those that rely more on existing knowledge and expectations than on the specifics of the text. Tasks that demand quite complex language processing in limited time are more challenging, and so particularly suitable for advanced learners.

3   **Use the text to improve reading strategies.** Authentic texts are likely to be particularly demanding in terms of unfamiliar words and patterns. So they provide a good opportunity for you to teach coping strategies, for example, by helping your learners to infer the meanings of unknown words and to use a dictionary where appropriate, for example to look up key words.

4 **Think about background knowledge.** Any reader needs appropriate background knowledge to interact effectively with a text. Think about what your learners might need to know about to appreciate the text you are offering them. How can you best activate the awareness they already have? And, if you think their awareness does not match the assumptions of the text's author, how can you bridge the gap?

5 **Look at the overall structure of the text.** Some text types have organizing patterns associated with them. Advertisements, for example, often point out a problem and then offer their product as a solution. Newspaper reports often begin with a very brief summary of the story that leaves out key details. They then go over the points again adding these details. If you are working with a particular text type and you can identify a typical pattern, share this with your learners. Knowledge of a text's pattern can make it easier to understand its language.

6 **Think about writer purpose.** Your text was produced to impart information, and also as part of a specific social relationship between writer and intended readers. By discussing probable writer purposes, you can increase learners' understanding of why a text is as it is, and this can help them to understand it better. For example, we might speculate that the newspaper writer referred to above has the purpose of attracting a reader to read the story (hence the brief summary), and then inducing the reader to read to the end – hence the withholding of key details!

7 **Look at how the text hangs together.** If you study it closely, you will find that certain key words and phrases are repeated again in sentences and paragraphs. This repetition contributes to the cohesion of the text. Writers also create cohesion by referring back to things they have mentioned before. By asking learners to look at these aspects of the text, you can raise their awareness of strategies that they may be able to use in their own writing.

8 **Look at vocabulary.** If you have selected a text from a specialist area, it may well contain vocabulary items that your learners particularly need to know. And either a specialist or a general text will contain examples of collocations – that is, words which typically go together. Some of these examples will be fixed lexical phrases, like *a long time ago* or *what it's all about*. By concentrating on these, you can give learners a new angle on how the language works.

9   **Look at tense use.** Especially in non-narrative text, writer choice – as opposed to language rules – determines a lot of tense use. This may come as a surprise to many learners who have learnt rigid ways of distinguishing the use of tenses from each other. Looking at tense use, and discussing possible alternatives, can help learners become more open-minded and receptive to the examples they see and hear.

10 **Consider creating a computerized mini-corpus.** The written texts you use can be stored on computer and then you and the learners can use a concordancing programme – a programme which shows some patterns which typically cluster around particular words – to study them. You can also add any transcribed spoken texts to your mini-corpus. By studying texts using a concordancer, learners can get information about some common language patterns – and they can begin to learn to do some of the research for themselves.

23

Exploiting authentic spoken texts

Our definition of the term 'authentic' needs to shift a little here. It can include texts from broadcast sources, produced for purposes other than language learning. But we'd also like to include as 'authentic' unscripted spoken texts that teachers themselves record – even if the situation was deliberately set up. The following suggestions should help you get the most out of using all kinds of spoken text.

1   **Decide what sort of text you want.** Are you looking for planned or semi-planned data (a TV speech, a radio interview), or spontaneous data – a chat between friends or colleagues? And are you looking for monologue or dialogue? Spontaneous dialogue can be particularly valuable because it is often under-represented in teaching materials, even though learners obviously need to cope with it in the world outside. But then, it is also the most difficult to record.

2   **Work with meaning first.** Let your learners hear the text in real time, and do something with it, before they look at its language in detail. One of the best ways of getting learners to work with meaning is to give them a good pre-listening task, which sets up a reason for listening and activates appropriate background knowledge.

3   **Address the difficulties of real time processing.** Listening is more difficult than reading because, unless learners are actual participants in the conversation, they cannot control the input – they cannot go back and hear bits again, or pause to work something out. So help them with strategies – such as listening for key words, noticing tone of voice – which will enable them to make the best of incomplete understanding.

4   **Make a transcript.** As well as meaning-focused activities, you will probably want to do some language-focused work. A transcript, of the whole of the text or part of it, is an essential aid for this – it will help both you and the learners really to notice the interesting features of the text and to compare and contrast different parts of it.

5   **Point out differences between spoken and written language.** If your learners have never seen spontaneous speech transcribed before they may be surprised at all the short language chunks, hesitations, fillers and 'ungrammatical' language. It is important for them to realize that these are normal and acceptable characteristics of unplanned speech. A short exercise where learners record and transcribe themselves speaking their own language can make this point well.

6   **Think about phonological features.** An authentic spoken text can be a good opportunity for learners to concentrate on one or two phonological features. You can use the text to raise their awareness of the way certain sounds are pronounced in context, or of the intonation patterns that speakers are using for a given purpose. This will be easier for learners when they have already worked with the meaning of a text.

7   **Look at openings and closings.** The beginnings and ends of exchanges can be especially difficult for learners to manage, because they tend to be quite ritualized and formulaic in different languages. You may be able to sensitize them to some standard ways of managing these transitions in English. Again, they can think about how openings and closings happen in their own language as a point of comparison.

8   **Look at the negotiation of (mis)understanding.** The meaning of a conversation is developed by the speakers as they go along. Sometimes the conversation may not go smoothly and the speakers have to renegotiate. It can be valuable for learners to look at how this is done, because they are likely to find themselves in similar situations.

9   **Look at how speakers collaborate.** Sometimes one speaker dominates a stretch of conversation, but the other is rarely passive. At the very least, the 'hearer' will be signalling their continuing understanding, and checking up on important points. If learners can become more aware of this, they will start to notice it in other conversations that they hear – their understanding and quite probably their own production will be improved.

10   **Spend some time on specific language features**. Spontaneous speech
      particularly is often full of prefabricated chunks: phrases such as, 'and
      the other thing was' or, 'that's funny, actually...' If learners become aware
      of these chunks they may start to incorporate them into their own speech,
      which can help them sound very fluent. Many of the specific language
      features mentioned in the section on written texts can be exploited with
      spoken texts, too. Vocabulary and tense use can both be profitably studied
      – it can be interesting to contrast usage in certain written and spoken
      texts.

24

Using literature

Literature can be a valuable addition to many courses even if it does not, strictly speaking, form part of learners' language study goals. It is part of the target culture, it can contribute to world knowledge, it engages readers emotionally and is enjoyable. The following tips should help you to use literary texts effectively with your learners.

1   **Select texts carefully.** For use in class, a text needs to be short: something you could read aloud in five minutes or less. Good candidates are poems, very short stories, or extracts from stories – though in this latter case, make sure the extract can actually stand alone. Also ensure that the complexity of the text is not too far outside your learners' range.

2   **Do preparatory work, if necessary.** Teaching one or two essential vocabulary items, or activating learners' knowledge of a context, can ensure that the text is globally understood on the first encounter. Such immediate understanding is highly motivating.

3   **Present the whole text before working on details.** You might read it aloud yourself – many literary texts are intended to be performed. You could also invite learners to read silently, if they have the experience to do so without worrying too much about details. The important thing is for them to feel the impact of the text as a whole.

4   **Build up understanding.** Ask learners for first reactions to the text. You can use a whole class format, inviting individual learners to contribute with anything they have understood or any reflections they have. This then forms a basis for rereadings and further work. The level at which they can engage after one reading/hearing gives you a good idea of how demanding the text will be for them.

5   **Ask learners to engage with the story.** Not all texts have stories, of course, but if yours does, you can ask learners to continue it, to express it from one character's point of view, or to think of a title which encapsulates it. All these activities raise awareness of the basic narrative and encourage involvement with the emotions of the text.

6   **Ask learners to interpret the text more deeply.** You could ask them to think about reasons for actions, viewpoints of characters, attitudes of characters or of the author, or the underlying message of the text. The goal here is a more critical engagement with the text.

7   **Use pair work for interpretative tasks.** Some of the suggestions above are difficult, even for intermediate or advanced level learners. You can set them the task in pairs, asking them to support any point they make with an example from the text. This gives them extra thinking time and the opportunity to practise what they want to say.

8   **Encourage learners to explore their personal response to the text.** Literary texts are after all intended to provoke a personal response, and some learners will be very keen to express it. This is an opportunity for a short writing activity – with lower level learners, such an activity could even be in L1.

9   **Consider language work.** Literary texts are also rich resources for grammar and vocabulary work. After learners have worked with the text as literature, they may like to explore elements of its language in a focused way. See 22, Exploiting authentic written texts.

10   **Encourage wider reading of literature.** Always tell learners where you got a text from, because some of them may want to carry on reading from the same book, magazine, etc. Be aware of local resources – ideally the school library or self-access centre – which they can use. See 31, Supporting self-access from the classroom.

25

Games for language learning

Language games are useful in many ways. They can help learners to practise pronunciation, develop vocabulary, extend their repertoire of communication strategies and try to produce humour in the target language. For teachers and learners alike, games can bring light relief and a change of pace to classes. The following ideas may provide you with some starting points to help you to design your own games for learners.

1 **Explain why you are using games.** Learners will get more out of language games if they can see the point of using them. Avoid the possibility of learners thinking that you are just wasting their time.

2 **Be prepared for different attitudes from learners.** Some learners will find the idea of using games weird, at least until they can see for themselves the benefits they are deriving from them. Some learners may be unduly competitive, not wishing to lose face by getting things wrong. Help all learners to see that one of the intentions is to have some fun, and that they should not take mistakes or errors seriously, but use them as learning experiences. The rest of the tips in this section give ideas for particular games.

3 **Who am I?** Choose a famous person, someone all of the learners are likely to have heard about. It is best if the person you choose is contemporary. Ask learners to try to find out who you 'are' by asking you questions, with yes/no answers, such as, 'are you male or female?', 'are you American?', 'are you a politician?', and so on. Then put learners into small groups, and ask them to take turns in choosing the personality.

4 **What's my line?** This is similar to 'who am I?' above, but focuses on particular job descriptions. Questions could include, 'is your work outdoors or indoors?', 'do you work with computers?', 'do you provide a service to people?', 'do you work with groups of people?', and so on.

5   **Animal, vegetable or mineral.** Everything except free space can be regarded as one or more of these. Allow a maximum of 20 questions (say) with which learners can probe the identity of the animal (including humans), or plant or object you have chosen. Then, when learners have found out how the game works, divide them into groups, and get them to take turns picking the object.

6   **Knockout quizzes.** Prepare a series of cards, each with a short question written on one side of it, and the answer written on the other side. Divide learners into teams, and deal out so many cards to each team. Ask each team in turn to select a question to pose to another team. If the other team answers correctly, they score a point and it is then their turn to pose a question. If the team does not answer correctly, the team posing the question scores a point, and can pose another question. With more advanced learners, you can get them to prepare the questions instead of doing it yourself.

7   **Crosswords or wordsearches.** You can get learners to devise these themselves. It is best to select a topic, such as food, or travel, or a particular building the learners all know. Then ask each group to exchange their crossword or wordsearch with other groups.

8   **Alphabetical circles.** Choose a topic, for example, shopping. The first learner could say, 'I went to the shop and bought an apple'. The next could continue, 'I went to the shop and bought and apple and a banana'. Then could come 'carrots', 'dates', 'eggs', and so on. It is normally best to use only 23 letters, as there are not many things starting with X, Y or Z.

9   **First and last letters.** For example, ask learners to call out the names of animals, where the next one starts with the letter that the last one finished with. Sequences, such as 'elephant', 'tiger', 'rhinoceros', 'seal', could result. The same process can be used for all sorts of topics themes, including countries, capitals, cities, and so on.

10   **Single letter mindmaps.** This is a quick game that you can play with a whole class at a time. Pick a topic beginning with a chosen letter, for example 'Danger'. Put this in a circle at the centre of a whiteboard or overhead transparency. Then build around it other words beginning with 'D' which link to the central topic. Examples for this one could be 'disaster', 'deep water', 'driving too fast', and so on.

11   **Homophones.** Draw a sketch of (say) a witch, and ask learners for another word (which) sounding the same as the word represented by the sketch. Then get learners in groups to take turns doing the same thing. They will need plenty of thinking time!

12 **Scrabble.** This commercially available game can be adapted for learners whose command of language is relatively high. Allow learners to use electronic spellcheckers, or the spellcheck facilities on computers (or, of course, dictionaries).

26

Role play

Role play, in some form or another, is a part of many contemporary language courses. Where learners are willing to enter into the spirit of role play, such activities provide a valuable opportunity for them to use their language resources creatively in a wide variety of imagined situations. Some people make a distinction between *simulation* – where learners are pretending to be themselves, but in a simulated situation – and *role play*, where they are pretending to be someone else. We use the term *role play* to cover both possibilities – it is up to you to decide which technique, or which combination of the two, is most appropriate for your learners. The following suggestions may give you some ideas upon which to base role play exercises for your learners.

1   **Set out to make role play fun.** Point out the benefits to learners in terms of opportunities for language use. Help them to see role play as a challenge, but not as a threat; don't come down heavily if they find it hard to be creative, especially at first. Then, as they get into the swing of things, discourage any tendencies for them to engage in role play too competitively.

2   **Keep role play relatively private.** It is best to carry out role play activities in twos and threes, and only to ask for public displays when you feel sure learners are ready. Let learners know in advance if you plan to ask some groups to show their work to the rest of the class, and choose groups who will be happy to perform.

3   **Let learners themselves choose which groups to work in.** Some learners will prefer to do role play activities in the comfort of single gender pairs or threes, or with their friends in the class. The more relaxed learners are, the more they will get out of role play activities.

4   **Provide clear briefings for planned role play activities.** Give details of the characters and scenarios in written form where appropriate. You can decide whether you want all the members of each group to know all these details, or whether you intend to spring some surprises.

5   **Give learners sufficient time to get into role.** Allow them time to make sense of the briefings and to tune in to the role that they are going to play. Give them time to think of ideas of their own that they will bring to their role play.

6   **Legitimize acting.** Encourage learners to bring some colour to the characters that they are going to play out. Distancing the characters from their real selves often helps learners to be more confident and relaxed in role play situations.

7   **Think of real situations that learners can role play.** These could include making a complaint to a shop manager, asking a noisy neighbour to be more considerate, and so on. Try to tap into situations where learners will have feelings of their own that they can act out.

8   **Get learners to extrapolate from a video extract.** For example, show a few minutes of a play or soap opera, which learners are familiar with, where learners have already been assigned roles of the characters involved. Stop the video at a suitable point, and ask groups of learners to fill out the next few minutes of the story for themselves. You may then find it useful to continue the video, so that learners can compare their versions with 'what actually happened'.

9   **Allow time for learners to get out of role.** It is important for learners to have time to look back at what happened in the role play, and to discuss what they learnt about communication and language. Get them to work out what they might have done differently, in the light of experience, if they were to tackle the same role play scenario for a second time.

10 **Get learners to devise their own role play scenarios.** They could then exchange these between groups, or you could use the best of them with a future group of learners. Composing the briefing details, and making sure that they are clear and unambiguous, is in itself a challenging and valuable activity.

27

Using the news

One way or another, the news is an important component of most people's lives. English language news, both live and print-based, is easily available in many countries and provides a wide ranging agenda for language development and communication skills practice. The following suggestions may help you to use 'the news' as a productive arena for your learners.

1 **Show the class a video of a five minutes news bulletin.** Then ask learners individually or in groups to write a set of headlines for a newspaper, based on the main points they have picked up from the bulletin. Don't worry if they can't follow typical headline 'style' – the important thing is for them to try to capture the essence of a news story in a few words.

2 **Get learners to make a commentary.** Give learners a short extract on an issue they know about, with the sound off. Get them to produce and rehearse a commentary that could accompany the video instead of the original sound track. They can try out their commentary live, and in real time, against the running video. It can also be worthwhile getting them to record their commentary on audiotape, and then to listen to it while watching the video again.

3 **Ask learners to compose subtitles for a videoed news bulletin.** Show the whole class a short extract from a news bulletin, then ask groups of learners to devise short messages which could communicate the main points of the bulletin to people who could not hear.

4 **News quizzes.** Play to the whole class a short radio news bulletin, then quiz groups of learners about the content of the bulletin. It is best to prepare the quiz in advance, and possibly print it out, so each team can write their answers against each question before scoring their work. You will soon find out about the best level for such quizzes; the level is appropriate when no team gets less than about half of the available points, and the winning team gets most answers correct.

5 **Cartoons and photos.** Get learners in groups to devise captions for well-chosen cartoons or photographs from a newspaper. You may then show them the original captions, or point out how many different valid ways there can be to describe a cartoon or photo.

6 **Have I got news for you!** Give learners some headlines from a newspaper, and ask them in groups to try to work out the likely story behind each headline. You could allow them to read the newspapers in advance for a few minutes. For learners with well-developed language skills, this activity can be turned into a fun game by asking learners to think of alternative, creative stories which may have matched the chosen headlines.

7 **Home/national news.** Ask learners to look for a news story current in their country, and to write and deliver aloud a two-minute summary of it designed for the UK media.

8 **Teletext pages.** Give learners a newspaper, and ask them to capture the essence of 10 or so main news items by turning each into a summary which could be contained on a single screen of teletext. Encourage them to keep sentences short and to the point. Suggest that they try to get the gist of each story into a well-chosen, short headline and the first sentence of the teletext page.

9 **Broadsheets and tabloids.** Encourage learners to read about the same story in both broadsheet and tabloid newspapers, and to discuss the differences of approach. Then invite them to select a different story from a broadsheet and turn it into the register of a popular or tabloid newspaper. Often tabloids are much harder for learners to understand than broadsheets, so you will need to choose a particularly accessible story for this activity.

10 **Radio bulletins.** Give learners copies of the front page of a newspaper, and ask them in groups to make a set of headlines for a short radio news bulletin. Then combine the groups, two at a time, and ask them to read out to each other their radio bulletins, and decide which one captured the news best, and why.

Chapter 4   Implementing Self-access

Self-access is an umbrella term that can be used to cover many kinds of guided independent learning. In certain well-resourced contexts, especially those where learners are both highly motivated and extremely busy, there is a tendency towards the design of language programmes where learners are asked to cover a significant amount of the syllabus outside the classroom. The plan may be for them to work in their homes, or in a self-access centre. This chapter offers some immediate suggestions on how to use and design independent learning materials. If your work includes independent learning as a major contribution to your courses, you may wish to explore the topic further, for example through *500 Tips on Open and Flexible Learning* (Phil Race, 1998) in the same series as the present book.

We start with some thoughts on how to set up a self-access facility from scratch. Much of this chapter is most relevant to those who have access to a reasonably large set of independent learning resources – but if you are in the process of introducing self-access into your context for the first time then this particular set of tips will help you.

We then look at the wide range of factors that you should consider in choosing and designing self-access materials for your learners. These sets of tips look at the principles underlying self-access material use, and are particularly relevant in contexts where independent learning is central to the course. We emphasize the importance of learning outcomes that match course aims, of engaging tasks, and of feedback.

We end with some considerations of the role of the teachers in supporting learners' use of self-access. We look first at things a class teacher can do to integrate the self-access and classroom-based strands of the learning experience. We then go on to look explicitly at the help that learners may need if they are to make the most of a self-access resource centre and its materials.

28

Setting up a self-access facility

Many large, well-resourced institutions have self-access centres, which you can encourage your learners to use, and that you can rely on if converting a part of your course to independent learning. But if you are working in a context where no self-access centre is available, you and your colleagues may wish to build up a smaller facility that can still provide some of the benefits of a formal centre in helping your students to broaden their range of learning skills. The following suggestions should help you to set up such a facility.

1   **Investigate possible premises.** Might a separate room be available for your facility? If so, you may be able to consider audio as well as print-based resources. If not, you will need to concentrate on a more portable facility to be used in existing classrooms.

2   **Investigate technical resources.** Will you have access to TVs, tape recorders or computers? The equipment available is obviously a key factor when deciding what sort of materials bank to build up.

3   **Start to collect source material.** A small facility could start with a series of printed texts, and audio texts if you have tape recorders. These texts will form the core of your self-access materials. You can start with just a few more texts than there are learners in the class, to give people the experience of choosing what to do and then swapping around.

4   **Try to get other colleagues to join you.** A group of teachers working together will build up a sizeable bank of materials much more quickly, and learners will benefit from the variety of approaches and ideas. A joint initiative by teachers could also impress school authorities, and they might make extra funds available to support your project.

5   **Develop a house style for materials writing.** It is the rubrics, tasks and comments that you build around the source texts that give the materials their 'feel'. Similarities of presentation, whether typographic (eg, always using the same typeface), or content related (eg, always starting with a statement of objectives), can be reassuring for learners, and help to present the self-access facility as a coherent project.

6   **State objectives clearly and relate feedback to these.** Statements of objectives make the purpose of the materials clear to the learners, and so help them to choose the right ones to work on. Feedback on the learners' tasks should also relate to these stated objectives: this is one good way of making sure that the tasks really are relevant and appropriate.

7   **Consider the idea of pathways.** As your bank builds up, look at how different materials relate to each other. Could you publicize 'sets' of materials on particular subjects, or sets which help to develop particular language skills? Grouping materials in this way helps learners to decide what to do and in what order.

8   **Discuss the role of the self-access facility with learners.** If they have not experienced self-access before, they will need to think about what it can contribute to their learning experience, and they will need to be supported in their early attempts to choose and use materials. Ongoing feedback and discussion is the best way to help learners to make the best use of the facility. See 31, Supporting self-access from the classroom, for further ideas here.

9   **Show learners what is available.** Open display systems such as wallcharts are the most helpful. They enable learners to see more or less at a glance what is available. Charts should include information about the topic of the materials and the language learning objectives they are intended to serve.

10 **Encourage learners to contribute to the facility.** If they have access to printed English texts outside the class, they may come across pieces that they think their classmates might like. Encourage them to bring such texts in, and enjoy the satisfaction of seeing their contributions 'written up' as proper self-access materials.

29

Choosing self-access materials

The notion that independent study may form a significant part of a language programme brings special challenges for the teacher to choose and design materials suitable for such study. There is a growing range of language learning resource materials commercially available that may be appropriate. The following suggestions may alert you to some of the things to look out for, to ensure that you select materials that will really help your learners to study effectively.

1   **Don't go for the first suitable looking materials that you come across.** If you are considering buying in multiple copies of materials, take time to make sure that you have made an informed decision about which package suits your needs best. If you are going to recommend that learners purchase their own copies of materials, it is important to ensure that they will be getting good value for money.

2   **Gather intelligence about the range of materials available.** Use your contacts in your own institution, and more importantly, in other places. This can be a faster way of tracking down suitable packages than simply searching through publishers' catalogues. Don't be taken in by some of the things that publishers may claim for their products; try to find someone whose judgement you trust and who has already used the materials before you decide to spend time working out whether it is what you are really looking for yourself.

3   **Investigate the intended learning outcomes of the materials.** Most good materials express these clearly at the beginning. The outcomes should be stated in language that learners themselves will relate to, rather than looking like a formal syllabus or course validation document. Check how closely the stated learning outcomes match the assessment criteria that you use on your programme. Then, as you explore the materials further, look carefully at whether the materials are really leading learners towards achieving the stated outcomes.

4 **Check that the materials are at the right level for your learners.** You may want to use them for central parts of your learners' work, or you could simply require them to use with learners who need some remedial development or practice. The intended learning outcomes should give some measure of the level of the materials, but it is worth looking at the actual level of the things that learners will *do* as they work through the package.

5 **Consider whether you might want to reformulate the learning outcomes.** For example, materials might be an effective learning tool, but may not have clearly articulated learning outcomes. Sometimes, materials come with learning outcomes that are written in teachers' terminology, and it can be useful to translate these into language that your learners will understand easily.

6 **Look at how well the materials make use of learning-by-doing.** Just reading through materials is of limited value, and is unlikely to bring about very deep learning. Materials should be leading learners into practice, and engaging their language resources via tasks, so that they can develop on their own their grasp of the various aspects of language that they are intended to work on.

7 **Look carefully at how learners receive feedback from the materials.** It is of little value getting learners to do exercises, if they are then unable to find out quickly how well (or how badly) they have done them. Well-designed, independent study materials are strong at giving learners feedback on their efforts. This is usually achieved by setting structured questions and tasks in the first place, for example, multiple-choice questions, so that separate feedback can be given as appropriate to learners who choose correct options from the feedback needed by learners whose choices are based on anticipated mistakes or misunderstandings.

8 **Look at the overall appearance of the materials.** This is less important than whether or not the package is educationally sound, but first impressions count with learners. If the materials look good (and *are* good), learners will trust them more, and value them more. If they look rough and ready, even if the content is good, learners may not feel they are as important and sound as if they looked more professional and polished.

9 **Try working through the materials yourself.** Even though you are likely to do all of the tasks and exercises correctly, and quickly, it is the best way to see for yourself how the materials are intended to work. You will sometimes find that materials that look good at first sight may fall in your estimation when you have found out more about what they actually entail for your learners.

10   **Pilot the materials with a few learners before you make a final decision to adopt them.** However hard *we* try to work out whether materials are good or not, the real test comes when learners work with them. One of the problems is that we tend to take for granted the process skills that independent learning materials demand: learners, especially those unused to this way of working, may find difficulties that we have not anticipated.

30

Designing self-access materials

There are many excellent materials for independent language learning available for purchase, but large self-access centres generally include a significant percentage of teacher designed materials. The advantages of this in terms of relevance and suitability for the learners concerned are obvious. Small or semi-formal facilities, perhaps without the benefit of an institutional budget, may rely entirely on teacher-designed materials. The following suggestions should help you to design independent learning materials suitable for your own course and learners; they also point out some of the benefits, for you, of doing this.

1   **Decide which elements of the course your learners may be able to study on their own.** For example, it is often helpful to use self-access materials to revise ideas with which your learners are already partially familiar. Those learners who are already up to speed can work through the materials quickly, while those who need to develop their skills or knowledge can work through the same materials in greater depth, and at their own pace, so that they gain the level of competence that you wish to use as a starting point.

2   **Look at what you've already got before starting to write self-access materials.** You will already have valuable resources that you use in face-to-face settings, including your own lesson plans, tasks and assignments that you set learners, handout materials, extracts from other source materials, and so on. You may be able to use such existing resources as a good starting point, building up self-access materials around them.

3   **Don't forget your most valuable assets!** These include your own knowledge of the target language, your knowledge of your learners, and your ability to respond to the most common problems that learners like yours experience. All of these are necessary starting points towards designing effective self-access materials.

4   **Start small.** It is better to design a number of small, self-contained activities, rather than to set yourself the task of adapting a large section of your course to independent learning all at once. After you've piloted and polished your smaller elements, it is relatively easy to integrate them together to make a larger package.

5   **Work out the intended learning outcomes for your materials.** Work out exactly what learners should be able to *do* after they have successfully completed each set of activities. Express these learning outcomes in clear, learner-friendly language. For example, 'when you've worked through this package, you should be able to...' is much more intimate and involving than 'the intended learning outcomes of this package are that students will be able to...'

6   **Focus hard on learning-by-doing.** Effective self-access materials are not just something for learners to read; they are something for them to work through. Try to structure the tasks and activities so that when learners have tried them, they can receive feedback on their attempts.

7   **Think feedback.** When structuring questions and activities, bear in mind that your materials should give learners the most specific feedback possible on the appropriacy of their answer. You need to be able to respond to what each learner has actually done. Open-ended questions are not amenable to this! Structured tasks, such as multiple-choice questions, allow you to respond separately to learners who have got the task right, as well as to learners who have chosen options representing different anticipated errors.

8   **Include open-ended tasks, too.** Their disadvantages in terms of feedback are more than outweighed by their advantages in terms of task authenticity and creative language use. Try to organize some class time for teacher and/or peer feedback on open-ended self-access tasks.

9   **Try out your tasks and feedback responses with live learners.** You can find out a lot about how well or badly your questions will work by watching learners trying them out. If they struggle or get stuck, find out why, and adjust the wording of questions and feedback until there is no longer a problem.

10   **Write the introduction to each piece of self-access material *last*.** The best time to write your lead-in to each set of activities is when you already know exactly what's in it, and how well it works. The introductions are particularly important when learners are studying on their own. There's no second chance to make a good first impression, and it is important to use each introductory section to whet learners' appetites for what is to follow.

31

Supporting self-access from the classroom

Many institutions today have the benefit of a large self-access centre which may contain highly sophisticated resources. Learners, then, require support to develop the skills which will enable them to make best use of a self-access centre. The following tips concentrate on what the class teacher can do to support learners' effective use of the self-access centre.

1   **Talk about the role of the centre throughout the course.** Learners who have not had access to such a centre before will be unsure how to use it and may even be suspicious, if they think it is intended to replace 'proper' teaching. You can help them to see it as a valuable complement to the taught course, and an excellent opportunity to develop independent learning skills.

2   **Organize a proper introductory session.** Many self-access centres have orientation sheets which take learners around the different areas of the centre, introducing them to various activities on offer. If your centre does not have one, write one which is suitable for your particular class.

3   **Encourage frequent use of the self-access centre.** The best way to do this is to make sure you know what's in there. You can then guide learners to appropriate – often short – activities, in response to issues arising in lessons.

4   **Integrate self-access and class work.** At appropriate intervals, ask learners to do self-access work to support what is happening in class. Give them a chance to feed back on what they did in the next lesson. In this way, you can continually demonstrate what is available in the self-access centre, and give the message that you find it of value.

5   **Hold occasional classes in the centre.** Many centres have a group work room, and this can be an ideal base for a project-oriented lesson where learners need to use the resources of the centre to find information for the project and then present it appropriately. Such a lesson gives you the chance to observe your learners using the centre, and to help them if they ask you to.

6   **Encourage independent self-access use.** When your learners are comfortable with the centre, they will be in a strong position to use it to follow individual learning agendas. You can help them to start to plan by means of informal questionnaires about interests and perceived areas of weakness, leading to suggestions for activities.

7   **Give learners the opportunity to report back on independent use.** One good way of doing this is a learner diary, where they might mention, among other things, what they did in the self-access centre. You can respond with encouragement, and perhaps suggestions. This is a good way of helping learners feel supported in their efforts.

8   **Get learners to write reviews of self-access activities.** These can then be displayed in the classroom. They act as information for other class members, and as continuing publicity for the centre. For example, to encourage extended reading you could ask learners to choose from the graded readers in the centre and to write comments on those they have read for other learners in the class.

9   **Encourage leisure activities, too.** Many self-access centres include magazines, videoed films and light reading, which could be seen by more advanced learners as relaxation rather than work. Reaching the stage where they can 'relax' in English boosts learners' self-esteem and contributes to their developing identity as proficient language users.

10 **Contribute materials to the centre.** Different institutions have different policies on this issue, but many welcome contributions from all the teaching staff. So if you come across material that you think would be useful, try to get it in there and build up the collection.

32

Training learners to use self-access materials

Some of your learners are likely to have worked with self-access materials successfully before and won't need much help regarding how to make best use of them. Learners who have not worked on their own before are likely to need study skills guidance. The following suggestions may help you to work out your own study skills briefing for learners using self-access materials (including ones that you have designed yourself, and ones you may have adopted or adapted).

1   **Explain the benefits to learners.** For example, they can learn-by-doing, at their own pace, and at times and places of their own choice. They can also choose whether to work through the materials entirely on their own, or whether to work collaboratively sometimes.

2   **Emphasize the advantages of the comfort of privacy in which to make mistakes.** Learners who don't like to be seen to make mistakes in class will appreciate the opportunity to practise with self-access materials, so that they can have as much practice as they like on particular concepts or skills.

3   **Help learners to make good use of expressed learning outcomes.** Explain that these are a frame of reference, allowing learners to see for themselves how their studies are progressing, and showing them what the expected targets and standards will be.

4   **Remind students of the value of learning-by-doing.** Explain to them that they will learn very little just by looking through self-access materials, and much more by having a try at each and every task and exercise. Point out that the heart of independent learning is the self-assessment which learners can do as they work through the materials.

5   **Help learners to make the most of the feedback in the materials.** Point out that there is nothing to be gained by looking at the answers or feedback after simply *reading* tasks, and that doing so is only robbing them of the value they could have gained by using the feedback after *doing* the tasks.

6   **Try to check up on whether learners are actually *doing* the tasks, questions and activities.** For example, ask them to bring along their marked-up copies of learning materials to class sometimes, where you can see what they have done. Ask learners to make lists of questions to ask you about any aspects of the learning materials with which they are having problems.

7   **Remind learners of their responsibilities.** Self-access can only make a meaningful contribution to a course if learners use it steadily over a period of time. The danger is that learners may not start using self-access materials, with other pressures on them to do coursework where it would be noticed if they did not do it. Encourage them to schedule regular time each week to work through their self-access materials, rather than leaving such work until they think it might be checked.

8   **Make sure that self-access is not seen as marginal by learners.** Clarify how the outcomes of independent learning will be assessed, and explain how the self-access materials contribute to the resourcing of the programme as a whole.

9   **Encourage learners to use particular sets of materials more than once.** The second time they work through such materials will take them much less time than their first attempt. However, if there has been a decent gap in between the result will be that they will find out for themselves which parts they have already mastered, and which parts warrant some extra attention.

10 **Design assignments based on the self-access materials.** These will help you to see how learners are progressing with the materials, and will also force learners into doing some work with them. More importantly, you will be able to see from learners' answers to the assignments if they have any problems with the independent learning elements of your course.

Chapter 5   Using Information and Communications Technologies

What are 'information and communications technologies'? Everything from computers, computer conferences, electronic mail (e-mail, or simply email) can be classified under this broad heading. In this chapter, we offer some suggestions that are central to your likely starting position regarding information and communications technologies. If this is a major area of your work, much more detail (in the same format and in the same series of books) is available in *500 Computing Tips for Teachers and Lecturers* (Phil Race and Steve McDowell, 1996) and *500 Computing Tips for Trainers* (Steve McDowell and Phil Race, 1998).

Information and communications technologies may be available to learners in their classroom, in a self-access laboratory situation or, indeed, in their homes. The nature and extent of their access will be an important factor in your decisions on how best to use information technologies with them. Perhaps a majority of our tips in this chapter assume at least a degree of out-of-class access.

We begin with some suggestions about getting learners started with e-mail. We assume that you are already using e-mail yourself – if you're not, then perhaps reading this set of tips will encourage you to get started. We then look at computer conferencing: for language learners, computer conferencing can be a powerful way of developing spontaneous written communication skills, in an environment where they can receive a great deal of useful feedback from each other, in the comfort and privacy of a seat at a computer terminal.

The range of computer-aided language learning packages is growing rapidly, and much may be available which would help your students to interact with English in stimulating and useful ways, provided, of course, that the availability of computers or terminals is sufficient to give them relatively unrestricted access to the learning packages. It is just as important to be really selective when choosing computer-based learning packages as it is when choosing print-based ones. We hope that our suggestions will alert you to some of the principal features that you will need to check out before committing yourself to purchasing a computer-based learning package.

Computer-delivered assessment is a more specialized area of information and communications technology, but it can pay huge dividends when adapted for providing students with learning-by-doing activities at a computer terminal, combined with immediate and useful feedback on-screen. It can, after an investment of your own time, also save you from some of the more routine burdens of marking learners' work when used in carefully selected areas of your teaching programme.

We end this chapter with some suggestions on how you can use e-mail to give feedback to learners. This can be beneficial to them as it is received in comfort and privacy, and it can help you by making it possible to harness the power of technology so that you don't have to write or speak identical feedback messages time and time again for different learners needing the same comments and advice.

33

Helping learners to get started with e-mail

The use of electronic mail has accelerated rapidly in the last few years. People who would not have been thought to be computer literate often take their first steps into the area because they are attracted by the benefits of e-mail. Many of your learners are likely to be up to speed with computers and e-mail, but the following suggestions may help you to whet the appetites of those who have not yet become 'mouse-trained'.

1   **Reassure learners that they are highly unlikely to break the computer!** For those learners who are reluctant to get into computer usage, there is often a concern that they may do something drastic and irreversible to expensive equipment. Remind learners that the only thing they are likely to risk when using computers is losing some of the work they have done with the machine, and even this risk is quite small, with 'undo' commands in most computer software, and with good habits of saving work to disk every few minutes.

2   **Explain the basic features of the e-mail system.** Show learners at least the subject line and the send, reply and forward functions. Make sure they all know your address and their own addresses. You can also show them how to make a group address for the class.

3   **Help learners to get started.** Probably the best way to do this is for you to *require* all of your learners to e-mail something short to you, with a time deadline. It can be worth thinking about using a short written exercise for this purpose, in which case you can attach at least some marks to the task. You could also send all your learners a message, to which they would need to reply. Ideas like this can make all the difference to learners who might otherwise not get round to finding out how to log in to the system and send an e-mail.

4   **Make learners' efforts worthwhile.** If you've asked all members of a class to e-mail something to you, try to respond *immediately* (within a day or two) to each message as it arrives. The fact that learners get a little individual feedback via e-mail from you, and that they get it quickly, helps them to see for themselves the potential of e-mail as a communication medium.

5   **Point out that e-mail is a way of practising spontaneous written communication skills.** Getting students to communicate with each other and with you using e-mail gives them an opportunity to use a written medium for relatively spontaneous communication. Attempting to write in the highly interactional, relatively informal medium of e-mail can make them more aware of strengths and weaknesses in their semi-planned language use.

6   **Promote the benefits of computer literacy.** The information technology revolution has meant that a much greater proportion of people need to use computers in their everyday work and lives. Being computer literate also means that people don't have to rely on other people to perform various tasks for them. For example, university-based learners who have mastered word processing don't have to pay someone to process their theses or dissertations, and can keep editorial control over them, making it much easier to change them whenever they receive some useful feedback about draft versions.

7   **Encourage learners to write using a word processing package before cutting and pasting into e-mail.** WP packages usually have much better editing facilities, including spelling and grammar check facilities. They allow learners to edit and polish their writing, so that *they* can have control over how spontaneous the e-mail message actually is. If learners were to attempt so much editing on a handwritten message, it could either look very messy, or have to be written out several times before the same amount of adjustments had been achieved.

8   **Remind learners that e-mail can be viewed as environment-friendly.** The saving of paper can be significant. If the computing facilities are already available, it can be argued that using e-mail incurs negligible costs.

9   **Encourage learners to write short e-mails!** One of the problems with e-mail communication is that people only tend to read the beginning of a message. If an incoming message is too long for immediate reading, people tend either to file them away for later reading (and forget them!) or simply delete them.

10   **Point out that e-mail communications are saved and kept on the system.** The exact way this happens varies between systems, but all e-mail users normally have at least an in, out and trash mailbox. It may also be possible to copy messages to personal files or disks. By whatever mechanism, learners can keep track of all the messages they have composed and sent. Keeping similar track of handwritten messages is less likely, or would involve the trouble and expense of photocopying. Learners looking back at a range of e-mails they have composed can see for themselves how their skills with the language are developing.

11   **Remind learners that e-mail can be a way of keeping in touch with friends in other institutions.** Most universities and colleges have Internet facilities available to learners, making it possible for them to send messages to anywhere in the world, let alone in the institution. Such facilities are normally free of charge to learners, and in any case the actual costs are insignificant once the equipment has been installed. You may be able to find English speaking 'keypals' for your learners through a local TESOL association.

34

Setting up computer conferencing

If your learners are people who would enjoy participating in debates, or group decision making/information building activities, or peer feedback activities, then it is worth considering doing these things via the medium of a computer conference. This can be set up in a particular class, or alternatively to serve particular needs of learners across a range of classes. The technicalities of how to set up the computer conference will of course vary according to particular systems available in different institutions, so we do not cover setup as such in these tips. But if the medium of computer conferencing is available to you, we hope our suggestions may help you to work out how to make the best use of it.

1   **Work out definite purposes for each computer conference.** Conferences are much more successful when they are provided to relate to identified needs, or specific intended outcomes. For example, it can be useful to use a computer conference as a vehicle for the creation of an annotated list of self-access resources by a class, helping students to learn from each other's work in tracking down relevant or useful materials.

2   **Explain to learners the benefits of participating in computer conferences.** Learners can exchange a lot of information, both study-related and social, through such conferences. They can get peer-feedback on their own ideas, and even on selected parts of their work. Participating in computer conferences helps learners to develop computer-related skills: for example, it can quickly help them to speed up their keyboarding skills.

3   **Consider allocating some coursework marks for participation in a computer conference.** This is one way of ensuring that all the learners in a class engage with a class conference. Once they have mastered the technique of contributing to a conference, most learners find that they enjoy it enough to maintain a healthy level of participation.

4 **Establish the extent of learners' access to networked terminals.** In particular, if contribution to a computer conference is linked to coursework marks, it is essential to ensure that learners cannot appeal against assessment decisions on the grounds of not being able to contribute due to lack of opportunity.

5 **Use computer conferences as a notice board.** A conference can provide you with a quick and efficient way to communicate detailed information to the whole of a class. Such information can include briefings for assessed tasks, hints and guidance about how to go about such tasks, as well as useful day-to-day information. Learners themselves can print off and keep anything that is particularly important to them.

6 **Think carefully about starter pages.** These are the introductory comments that learners read when they log into the conference, and to which they append their replies. Each starter page should have a definite purpose, so that replies and ensuing discussion are focused rather than rambling.

7 **Aim to get the essence of a starter page on to a single screen of information, or less.** If learners have to scroll down more than one page before finding out what is being addressed and how they can join in, they are less likely to read the starter page and, therefore, less likely to start contributing to the conference.

8 **Choose the titles of starter pages carefully.** If you have more than one computer conference going, the titles of starter pages are likely to appear on your computer system as an index, in the order in which the pages were originally entered. Aim to make these titles self-explanatory, so that learners can tell what each conference is about from the directory, rather than having to read the whole of a starter page before finding out whether they wish to explore the topic further.

9 **Don't cover too much in a starter page.** It is better if each conference is relatively self-contained, and prescribed, rather than having topic pages which cover several different aspects. As new matters arise from learners' replies to starter pages, decide whether to introduce new starter pages/ conferences to carry these matters forward separately. Add your own responses to direct learners, who may be following the conference themes, regarding where in the conference each theme is being developed further.

10   **Vet computer conferences rigorously.** For example, remove anything offensive or inappropriate before it is likely to be seen by many learners. If particular learners misuse the conference, treat the issue seriously and seek them out and warn them of the consequences of such actions, for example, loss of computer privileges or even suspension from the course. The process of controlling a computer conference is often known as *moderation*; it is useful to recruit student moderators from those learners who are particularly computer-literate, and who may be only too willing to become conference moderators, editing and re-arranging contributions to keep the structure of the conference fluent and easy to follow.

35

Choosing computer-aided learning packages

As other tips in this chapter reflect, we are at a point where the integration of electronic materials into teaching–learning situations seems ever more possible. Learning and reference packages are being put on to the market in increasing numbers, and many teachers have the knowledge, interest and facilities to create their own teaching/learning software. Here we will look at factors to consider when choosing computer-aided learning packages. Many of the suggestions given elsewhere in this book about selecting print-based learning packages continue to apply when choosing computer-based ones. Some of our suggestions relate to packages that you might use in a class, others to out-of-class use. We hope our suggestions will help you to select appropriate packages for your particular learners.

1   **Choose your packages carefully.** Read a good review, for example in an educational software journal, of any package you are considering buying. Journals can raise your awareness of new packages, as well as give information about those you are already aware of! You can also ask the supplier or manufacturer for details of clients who have already used particular packages, and check that the packages really deliver what you need.

2   **Find out about packages from colleagues in other institutions.** Use your contacts. Ask them about packages they know of that work well and really help students to learn. Also ask them about packages that they don't rate highly, and about the factors that led them to this conclusion.

3   **Consider packages that are not specifically designed for language learning.** Anything that requires decision making, such as a 'dungeons and dragons' type game, can provoke valuable discussions if learners do the activities in small groups. Children particularly might enjoy working with packages designed to develop other cognitive skills, such as maths skills, through the medium of English.

4   **Try before you buy.** Computer-aided learning packages can be quite expensive, especially if you need to purchase a site licence to use them on a series of networked computer terminals, or to issue learners with their own copies on floppy disk. The best indicator of a good package is evidence that learners engage with it and are appropriately stretched by it. If you're considering buying a particular package, try to get a sample of your learners to evaluate it for you. They can then give you feedback on their experience of using it.

5   **Get familiar with the package, before giving it to your learners.** There is a learning curve to be ascended with most computer-based packages, and it is best if *you* go up this ahead of your learners. They will need help on how to make best use of the package, as well as on what they are supposed to be learning from it. Find out what it feels like to use the package. By far the best way to do this is to work through the package yourself. Find out what learners will *do* as they use the package, and check whether the tasks and activities are really relevant to your learners, and pitched at an appropriate level for them.

6   **Check the intended learning outcomes of the computer-based package.** The best packages state the intended learning outcomes clearly within the first few screens of information. Alternatively, the intended outcomes may be spelled out in supporting documentation, which comes with the package itself. Check that they are appropriate and that the package actually matches them.

7   **Think about access to equipment and software.** It can be prohibitively expensive to give or loan each learner both the software and the hardware needed. However, if the package is an important part of their overall programme, ways need to be found to maximize their opportunity to work with it. Some packages come with licence arrangements to use the package with a given number of learners, either allowing multiple copies to be made, or the package to be used over a network. Ensure that the software is protected in order to prevent unauthorized copying, or unlicensed use on more than one machine.

8   **Check that learners will get adequate feedback on their work with the package.** One of the main strengths of computer-based learning packages is that learners can be given instant feedback every time they select an option in a multiple-choice question, or key in a word or phrase, and so on. The feedback should be much more than just the correct answer to the question or task. Learners who get it wrong need to find out from the programme *why* their answer or response was wrong, and exactly *what* was wrong about it.

9   **Check how long activities and pathways within the package should take.** The time spent by learners should be reflected in the learning payoff they derive from their studies with the package. Many computer-based learning packages indicate the expected timescales that are involved in using them, but it is well worth finding out how long typical learners actually take. Also find out whether a game, for example, can be saved to continue later – it is very frustrating for learners who have to quit a package part way through an activity to have to start again from the beginning next time.

10   **Think ahead to assessment.** Work out what will be assessed, relating directly to the learning that is to be done using the computer-based materials. Express this as assessment criteria, and check how these link to the intended learning outcomes. Make sure that learners, before working through the computer-based materials, know *what* will be assessed, *when* it will be assessed and *how* it will be assessed.

11   **Explore software that tracks learners.** Many computer-based materials can be used to track individual learners' progress through them. This can involve pre-testing and post-testing, and storing the data on the computer system, as well as monitoring and recording the time taken by each learner to work through each part of the package. Such data can be invaluable for discovering the main problems that learners may be experiencing with the topic, and with the package itself.

12   **Seek feedback from your learners.** Ask them what aspects of the package they found most valuable and most important. Ask them also what, if anything, went wrong in their own work with the package. Look at the feedback you obtain for anything that throws light on particular categories of learners finding difficulties with learning from the package (for example, mature learners, or those with least time available to study, or people who are uncomfortable with new technologies). Be sensitive to the needs of those who may prefer *not* to work with a computer.

36

Designing computer-delivered assessment elements

Computer-delivered assessment can be used to reduce the burden of some kinds of routine marking of learners' work. It can also be used to give learners immediate feedback on their answers to structured questions. Some contemporary packages allow authoring facilities, so that you can add your own texts, make assessment questions and input feedback, and decide what is to appear on particular screens; many of our suggestions assume that you are working with this type of software. We hope the suggestions will help you to see where computer-delivered assessment could fit into your work.

1   **Work out which areas of language may lend themselves to computer-delivered assessment.** Such assessment is possible where it is straightforward to design structured questions, particularly multiple-choice ones. This requires there to be a correct (or best) option (referred to as the key), and other incorrect (or less good) options called distractors.

2   **Check carefully that the correct option really *is* correct.** If there is anything at all doubtful about the correct answer to a multiple-choice question, the most able learners in particular are likely to be thrown. Also check that there is not the possibility of one of the distractors being arguably correct, too.

3   **Look at the class exercises that you already use.** Many of the written exercises will contain elements which lend themselves to computer-delivered assessment. It is particularly useful to consider packaging up straightforward questions, which you often use, to save you time (and boredom) in marking learners' answers by hand.

4   **Look at the most common mistakes made by learners in existing tests or exercises.** It is often possible to turn these mistakes into distractors in computer-delivered multiple-choice tests. This means that you have the

chance to allow learners to make these anticipated mistakes, then use the computer to give them immediate feedback, which is a useful supplement to the feedback from tutor-marked work.

5   **Consider using computer-delivered tests for feedback only, rather than assessment.** While the computer programs may normally be used for testing and keeping learners' scores, it is easy to disable the scoring if you wish to do so, and to design tests simply to exploit the benefit of learners getting immediate feedback on their answers.

6   **Don't forget to use a few words of praise for learners who answer a question correctly.** Simply saying 'good' or 'well done' provides useful positive feedback to learners, and the computer doesn't get tired of repeating such words or phrases.

7   **Be gentle with incorrect answers.** Learners who pick an incorrect option may need reassurance. They also may need help in seeing *why* their option was incorrect, and not just to be told what the correct (or best) option would have been. Don't resort to the default feedback provided by the computer program, which may be as blunt and unhelpful as 'your answer is wrong; the correct answer is ...'

8   **Help learners to consolidate their learning.** When feedback is being provided on-screen, it is particularly helpful to learners if they can still see the question and the options from which they made their selection, while reading your feedback to the option that they selected.

9   **Consider using a printout of the test, and the feedback.** Many computer-delivered assessment packages can be programmed to provide a printout for each learner of all of the questions, along with feedback on the options they selected, as well as an overall result and feedback on their overall performance. It is useful for learners to have something they can look at again, when they are not at the computer or terminal.

10 **Make the most of the software.** It may be possible to programme the software to keep records for each learner, and for a whole class, and to print out class performance lists. It may also be possible to get the software to analyse the performance of each individual question and option. The software can work out the facility value of each question, showing which questions proved to be easy or hard in general. It can also compute the discrimination index of each question, showing which questions are best at separating the more able learners from the less able ones.

11 **Pilot your tests or exercises well.** Each time you run a particular computer-delivered test or exercise, you can normally learn a lot about how the questions, options and feedback can all be fine-tuned and polished. It is then possible to edit and improve the test or exercise.

12 **Use computer-delivered tests or exercises to gather feedback from learners.** For example, you can set a few multiple-choice questions to ask learners what they think about the test or exercise (not scoring such questions of course). You may be surprised to find out how much learners like the computer-delivered format, particularly if they find your feedback comments helpful and relevant.

37

Giving learners feedback using e-mail

E-mail is particularly useful as a vehicle for giving learners individual feedback on tutor-marked work. The following suggestions may help you to exploit the benefits of e-mail, not least to save you time and energy in giving learners feedback.

1   **Make the most of the comfort of privacy.** When learners receive feedback by e-mail (as opposed to face-to-face or in group situations), they have the comfort of being able to read the feedback without anyone seeing their reactions to it. This can be useful when the feedback is complex, and there is a lot of information to take in. It can also be useful when the feedback is critical; although sometimes written criticism can sound very cold. You will need to judge when it would be more appropriate to ask a learner actually to see you about a particular piece of work.

2   **Remember that you can edit your own feedback before you send it.** For example, you may well want to adjust individual feedback comments in the light of that learner's overall performance. It is much harder to edit handwritten feedback on a learner's written work. E-mail feedback allows you to type in immediate feedback to things that you see in each learner's work, and to adjust or delete particular parts of your feedback as you go further into marking their work.

3   **Exploit the space.** Inserting handwritten feedback comments into learners' written work is limited by the amount of space that there may be for your comments. With e-mail feedback, you don't have to restrict your wording if you need to elaborate on a point.

4   **Consider combining e-mail feedback with written feedback.** For example, you can write on to learners' work a series of numbers or letters, at the points where you wish to give detailed feedback. The e-mail feedback can then translate these numbers or letters into feedback comments or phrases, so that learners can see exactly what each element of feedback is telling them. The fact that learners then have to decode each feedback element may help them to think about it more deeply, and learn from it more effectively, than when they can see the feedback directly on their work.

5   **Spare yourself from repeated typing.** When designing computer-delivered feedback messages, you should only have to type each message once. You can then copy and paste all of the messages where you need to give several learners the same feedback information. It can be useful to combine this process with numbers or letters, which you write on to learners' work, and building up each e-mail to individual learners by pasting together the feedback messages which go with each of the numbers or letters.

6   **Consider the possibilities of 'global' feedback messages.** For example, you may wish to give all of the learners in a large group the same feedback message about overall matters arising from a test or exercise. The overall message can be pasted into each e-mail, before the individual comments addressed to each learner.

7   **Check that your e-mail feedback is getting through.** Most e-mail systems can be programmed to send you back a message saying when the e-mail was opened and by whom. This can help you to identify any learners who are not opening their e-mails. It can also be useful to end each e-mail with a question asking the learner to reply to you on some point arising from the feedback. This helps to make sure that learners don't just open their e-mail feedback messages, but have to read them!

8   **Keep records of your e-mail feedback.** It is easy to keep copies on disk of all of your feedback to each learner, and you can open a folder for each learner if you wish. This makes it much easier to keep track of your ongoing feedback to individual learners, than when your handwritten feedback is lost to you when you return their work to them.

9   **Make the most of the technology.** For example, some e-mail systems support spellcheck facilities that can allow you to type really fast and ignore most of the resulting errors, until you correct them all just before sending your message. This also causes you to reread each message, which can be very useful for encouraging you to add second thoughts that may have occurred to you as you went further in your assessment of the task.

10   **Use e-mail to gather feedback from your learners.** Learners are often bolder sitting at a computer terminal than they are face-to-face. Ask your learners questions about how they are finding selected aspects of their studies, but don't turn it into an obvious routine questionnaire. Include some open-ended questions, so that they feel free to let you know how they are feeling about their own progress and about your teaching, too.

Chapter 6   Assessment

Assessment can be described as the engine that drives students' learning. The fact that, in many contexts, students are becoming more strategic means that assessment can be harnessed to help them to focus their learning, as well as to measure the level they have reached. If you wish to read from a cross-disciplinary perspective on the different kinds of assessment you may wish to choose from, please look at *500 Tips on Assessment* (Sally Brown, Phil Race and Brenda Smith, 1995), where a much wider range of assessment formats is addressed.

Our chapter on assessment begins and ends with testing. The primary benefit that learners can reap from testing is feedback, so the design of a classroom test should be regarded as paving the way for learners to deepen their learning from feedback on anything they get wrong, rather than trying to find out how many learners can get things right.

We also include some suggestions for involving learners in their own assessment. Self-assessment can bring the comfort of privacy to finding out about strengths and weaknesses. Peer-assessment can extend the amount of feedback that learners receive, and deepen their learning through the process of applying assessment criteria to someone else's work. Both self- and peer-assessment can help learners to tune in to the assessment culture in which they are learning English, and can help them to see how the examiner's mind will work when assessing their work when it counts.

Our final suggestions in this chapter point towards helping your learners to succeed in public exams, where you may need to join forces with your learners to help them to adjust their strategic preparations in the most sensible ways.

38

Designing classroom tests

A formal classroom test is one of the many options available if you want to assess your learners' progress and achievement. In many institutions, formal tests are highly valued and everyone expects that teachers will use them. The following suggestions should help you to design small-scale tests that allow your students to show what they have learnt, and which fit easily with the styles of teaching and learning which are present in your classroom.

1   **Make your test representative rather than exhaustive.** Look back through your lesson notes to see what the teaching goals have been in the period leading up to the test, and then draft questions which relate to those goals. This is a good way of ensuring content relevance, without trying to cover every detail of the teaching programme.

2   **Use activities that you use in class.** For example, if you sometimes ask your learners to reorder jumbled paragraphs to form a coherent text, also consider this activity for your test. Learners will do better on activities they are familiar with, and they will also be encouraged to see the links between the test and the wider learning experience.

3   **Avoid unfamiliar question formats.** Sometimes it's tempting to choose the question formats we see in public exams, especially if they're quick and easy to mark. Some people feel that these formats lend authority and objectivity to classroom tests. But if the test formats are not representative of the way you teach, they may not provide valid information about your learners' progress in class.

4   **Get a colleague to check your question paper.** It is all too easy to write instructions that are not clear, or 'objective' questions where there is actually more than one right answer. A colleague can often spot problems like this. It's especially important to check the question paper in settings where the learners will be expected to take the test in silence, without further help from the teacher.

5   **Make your test criterion-referenced.** For each question or task, have a specific idea of what learners must do to gain marks. Make sure the criteria relate to what you've done in class. If this means that many learners get similar, high marks, so much the better – this shows that testing and learning are working together.

6   **Use mark schemes where appropriate.** Mark schemes are an important part of criterion referencing for subjectively marked questions, such as letter writing tasks or oral interactions. If you write down the expected characteristics of performances at different levels, and refer to the guide when marking, you are less likely to find yourself marking simply by impression. Impression marking tends to lead to learners being compared with each other, rather than with the test criteria.

7   **Help your learners to prepare well.** Tell them in advance when the test will be, and tell them about the likely content, question types and marking criteria. Learners are more likely to learn from test preparation if they can be confident that their efforts are appropriately directed.

8   **Give detailed feedback, promptly.** If the test is to be part of the learning experience, learners need specific advice about where they did well and where they did less well. And this feedback is likely to be most effective if it is given when the test experience is still fresh in the learners' minds, and when they are anxious to know how they got on.

9   **Involve learners in marking where you can.** For 'objective' questions, with one correct answer, it is relatively simple to involve learners in marking their own or their classmates' papers. As you lead a discussion as to why various alternatives are or are not acceptable, learners are encouraged to think more deeply about the language being tested.

10   **Keep it short!** Classroom tests will probably happen quite frequently. So short, representative tests help to ensure that test preparation, administration and feedback do not come to dominate the whole of the teaching–learning experience.

39

Giving feedback on classroom tests

Students can learn a great deal from feedback on tests, but this depends very significantly on how and when the feedback is delivered, and on how well the learners themselves are able to receive the feedback. The following suggestions should help your learners to optimize the benefits that feedback on classroom tests can bring them.

1   **Give feedback as soon as possible.** Feedback works best when learners can still remember what they were trying to do in the test. In particular, when learners have made mistakes, give them feedback so quickly that they can still remember the possibilities they were weighing up when they made their decisions in the test.

2   **Help learners to see that feedback is valuable.** It is useful to make sure that learners are aware of how much they can learn from feedback. Ideally, learners should *want* to have feedback on everything they do, both to find out what they are doing well, and to diagnose areas upon which to concentrate further efforts.

3   **Help learners not to shrug off positive feedback.** In many cultures (not least English-speaking ones), there is a tendency to be embarrassed by positive feedback. Learners (and others) often don't receive the full benefit of feedback on things that they have done well, due to their tendency to dismiss praise. Help learners to see that taking ownership of things that they have done well is an important step towards being able to continue to do them well.

4   **Help learners to receive critical feedback.** All critical feedback should be constructive, showing learners not just what was wrong with their work, but what steps they can take to overcome the particular weaknesses or problems that were involved. In particular, learners need to know *why* their own efforts may have been incorrect or problematic.

5   **Be aware of learners' feelings.** For example, written feedback in red pen is immediately off-putting, even if the feedback is entirely positive. Also, words like 'failed', 'have not understood...', 'did not grasp...', 'disappointing', and so on, have obviously damaging effects on learners' morale, and can close them down regarding their reception of your feedback.

6   **Use a combination of written and oral feedback.** Both kinds of feedback have their advantages and their limitations, and to make feedback as effective as possible it is useful to use both tools to make the feedback as comprehensive and relevant as possible.

7   **Exploit oral feedback for the human warmth it can deliver.** Face-to-face feedback can bring tone-of-voice, facial expression, smiles, as well as the chance to monitor the effect that the feedback is having on learners, and to adjust the delivery of further feedback accordingly. The danger is that learners only remember particular parts of oral feedback, and may (for example) only remember the bad news, and dismiss or forget important good news.

8   **Exploit the permanence of written feedback.** Written feedback can convey both good and bad news. The record is permanent, which means that learners can revisit both kinds of news about their work. At the same time, it is particularly important to deliver any bad news in a kind and sensitive way when using written feedback, otherwise learners' morale and motivation can be permanently damaged.

9   **Get feedback on your feedback processes!** Find out how learners prefer to receive feedback on their work. Expect to discover that some learners find oral feedback most useful, while others benefit more from written feedback, and where possible accommodate learners' own preferences.

10   **Find out about your learners' feedback agendas.** Ask your learners what feedback they would particularly like. Sometimes you will find that they would like feedback going beyond your perception of their feedback needs. Giving learners feedback on things they have asked for increases their sense of ownership of the feedback agenda, and helps them to receive both positive and critical feedback more effectively.

40

Getting learner self-assessment going

Students can learn a great deal from self-assessment. It is important not to mix up learner self-assessment and learner peer-assessment; both processes pay dividends, but they are quite different. The following suggestions aim to give you some ideas on how you can put learner self-assessment to optimum use in your programmes.

1   **Self-assessment does not have to 'count'.** Many teachers are afraid to introduce learner self-assessment, in case there should be allegations that learners are being too generous to themselves, compromising the reliability of the assessment. (In practice, in fact, most studies show that if anything learners tend to be over critical, not over generous, when assessing their own work). Beginning self-assessment as a developmental process only, without it contributing to a final mark, can be reassuring both for learners and for the school administration.

2   **Self-assessment is an excellent way of alerting learners to what is important.** Applying assessment criteria to their own work helps learners to see how assessors' minds work, and helps them to tune their work to match what is being looked for by assessors.

3   **Train learners in self-assessment.** It is worth doing at least one or two whole class exercises, then facilitating learner self-assessment, so that any learners who are uncertain how best to go about measuring their own work can be helped. Such exercises can also help to convince learners that their own self-assessment can be just as accurate and valuable as assessment by an expert, such as a tutor.

4 **Be ready for '...but *your* job is to assess my work.'** Some learners may hold the view that assessment is nothing to do with them. This is partly a question of educational culture, and you will need to be sensitive about the appropriacy of an innovation like self-assessment. However, you may be able to win learners over, by alerting them to how much they can learn from measuring their own work, and reassuring them that you will still be assessing it, too, but that you will be able to help them all the more when you see their own perceptions of how their work is progressing.

5 **Self-assessment can be done in the comfort of privacy.** It is useful to get learners to self-assess some of their own work without having any inquest or debriefing. This allows learners to note areas of weakness without anyone else being aware of them, and to address these areas privately before undertaking more public kinds of assessment.

6 **Explore the benefits of a self-assessment tutor dialogue.** For example, get learners to self-assess exercises or tests before handing them in, and then give them feedback on the precision of their self-assessment. This is a good way of finding out those areas where learners lack awareness, and working out what to do to help learners to address such areas.

7 **Use self-assessment to speed up *your* assessments.** Particularly with the assessment of learners' written work, it can be much faster to mark work that learners themselves have already self-assessed, than to mark 'raw' exercises or tests. It becomes easier to identify those areas where learners really need feedback from you and, for example, to plan further exercises to address issues that are causing most learners some difficulty.

8 **Allow self-assessment to deepen learning.** It is highly productive to get learners themselves to work out what was good and what was problematic in their own work. This, at the very least, helps them to reflect on everything that they have done in a test or an exercise. At best, learners self-assessing often then see what they could have done to avoid mistakes. They then have the sense of ownership of such discoveries, and can be much more likely to build on this ownership than if someone else had assessed their work.

9 **Help learners to develop a culture of self-assessment.** Learners who have become accustomed to the processes of self-assessment are able to extend them into their revision strategies. Revision is better focused if learners are continuously measuring their own performance, rather than trying to prepare for the unknown.

10   **Consider *sometimes* coupling learner self-assessment with peer-assessment.** Although self-assessment is essentially quite different from peer-assessment, it is useful for learners to have some opportunities to compare the ways they are self-assessing their work with fellow learners. A way of bridging the gap is to use the occasional task or exercise that is first self-assessed, then peer-assessed, and to get learners to look for the things that they learnt from any differences that arose between the two approaches.

41

Getting learner peer-assessment going

Peer-assessment can be particularly useful for language learning, because it is in itself a demanding and multifaceted communication task. The following suggestions may alert you to ways in which you might choose to build on the benefits of peer-assessment.

1   **Use peer-assessment as a way of getting more feedback to learners.** This can include feedback on both oral and written exercises. If the ability range of the group is mixed, you may need to ensure that learners don't always receive feedback from the same peers, so that the feedback given by the most able learners is shared around the whole group.

2   **Explain the benefits of peer-assessment to learners.** It is important that they don't feel that peer-assessment is a cop out on your part! Explain to them that peer-assessment means that they get *more* feedback than you would have been able to give them yourself, and that you will then be able to concentrate on giving them feedback about really important aspects of their learning.

3   **Remind learners of the benefits of explaining things to each other.** Explaining a difficult area is one of the best ways of helping the learner who is actually trying to explain it, to make sense of the issue. Putting things into words helps learners to get their own minds around ideas and concepts. On the receiving end, having something explained by a fellow learner can be less intimidating than when a tutor is doing the explaining.

4   **Make the assessment criteria really clear.** When assessing learners' work yourself, you will probably do much of your assessment against criteria that are clear in your mind, but not written down in any detail. For learners to be able to peer-assess well, they need a firm briefing about what they should be looking for, and elements that should score marks as well as lose them.

5   **Consider getting the learners themselves to formulate the criteria for peer-assessment.** Ask learners, in groups, to work out a marking scheme for a task or exercise, and to put marks against criteria that they would be looking for while assessing each other's work. Get each group to display their criteria to the whole class, and justify the weighting they have awarded different elements of their schemes. Then help the learners to choose an overall peer-assessment scheme which reflects each of the group products. Aim for the whole group to have a sense of ownership of the final peer-assessment criteria.

6   **Think about when the peer-assessment criteria should be generated.** When the criteria are generated *before* learners undertake the task that is going to be peer-assessed, learners can keep the criteria in mind as they work, and the quality of their work is better. Alternatively, working out peer-assessment criteria *after* learners have undertaken a task tends to lead to sharper criteria, as they know what they tried to achieve in the task.

7   **Consider using peer-assessment to cover more ground.** For example, set a range of peer-assessed tasks, so that learners are all assessing something that they have not done themselves. This causes the class as a whole to do more thinking and practising, and to become aware of any gap in their own language resources.

8   **Assess alongside learners who are peer-assessing.** If, for example, learners are peer-assessing each other's presentations, it can be useful for you to assess alongside them, using the same criteria. When learners see that the average of their assessment is close to yours, their confidence in peer-assessment increases, and they become more willing to enter into it fully in future.

9   **Moderate and adjudicate as necessary.** You may find that it is much quicker to *moderate* a large pile of peer-assessed written work than to mark it from scratch yourself. You will soon be alerted to the particular learners whose peer-assessing is too lenient or too harsh, and can adjust accordingly. You will also quickly pick up the points that you may want to give feedback on to the whole class.

10 **Consider awarding some marks for the quality of peer-assessment.** If, for example, learners are peer-assessing something which counts for 20 marks, think about giving each learner a further five marks for peer-assessing really well, and asking the learners whose work has been peer-assessed to make the first decision about how many of these marks have been earned, then moderate this yourself. The fact that there are marks attached to the process of peer-assessing is normally enough incentive to help learners to approach the task more earnestly.

42

Preparing learners for public examinations

Many of us are teaching in a context where our students' language learning will be assessed via an external examination. Indeed for some learners, the goal of passing an exam is in fact the main motivation for attending classes. These suggestions should help you to respond both to the broad goal of helping students to learn more and more effectively, and to the specific goal of helping them to pass their target exam.

1   **Familiarize yourself with the exam syllabus.** Many exam boards provide information about the language content and processes which might be tested in a particular exam. They also provide information about the text-types most usually used for input, and about marking criteria. Getting a picture of the principles behind an exam is the first step in deciding how to prepare for it.

2   **Familiarize yourself with the question formats.** In many modern exams, the line between test content and test method is blurred, so that the question formats might represent specific language skills that your learners need to acquire. And if learners are familiar with the question formats, they will feel more confident and, therefore, perform better when they come to take the exam.

3   **Get hold of examiners' reports for previous years.** These give invaluable insight into how marking criteria are actually used, and into the standards examiners expect. They may include extracts from the performance of previous candidates, which you could look at with your own learners.

4   **See if there is a coursebook associated with the exam.** Well known, international exams do tend to spawn coursebooks. You will need to choose carefully; they vary in approach and quality, and some have been criticized for not actually matching their target exam very well. But by evaluating and being selective, you will probably find useful material.

5   **Be creative about exam practice.** It's often appropriate to use an exam-focused coursebook or even past exam papers in class. But you may need to adapt these if they are also to function well as teaching materials. For example, could you personalize any of the activities? Then your learners will still be practising for the exam, but they will also be learning to talk about their own lives, which is more valuable in the long run.

6   **Encourage collaboration during practice.** Some exam questions – even 'objective' questions – could be adapted for learners to work on in pairs or groups. This gives them an opportunity to discuss what language is most correct or most effective as an answer. The discussion process encourages reflection and, therefore, deeper learning.

7   **Share mark schemes with learners.** Where test questions (for example, writing tasks) have mark schemes, show these to your learners. Help them to understand the concepts, even if the language of the mark scheme is difficult for them. Encourage them to evaluate their own work using the marking criteria.

8   **Record your learners' oral performance.** If the exam includes speaking tasks, record your learners as they practise one of these. Play the recording back, and discuss it. This will sharpen learners' awareness of those features that get good marks in exams.

9   **Let learners see their progress.** Later in the course you can record the same speaking task again, and compare the two recordings. It is motivating for learners to see how they are progressing. It also helps them to see that language learning is not just learning to do more things; it can mean learning to do the same thing better.

10   **Don't lose sight of the whole educational experience.** A good course will continue to be valuable to learners long after the exam has been taken. So help them, at appropriate times, to focus on their wider educational aspirations; and also keep focusing on your own.

Chapter 7   Personal and Professional Development

Parts of this chapter are about your own continuing professional development, and other parts are about your survival!

First we look at ways of continuing to educate yourself in TESOL. Reading professional journals is an important way of keeping up to date with, and reflecting critically upon, developments in our field. If you want further tips on following up the last suggestion in this set, try *500 Tips for Getting Published* (Sally Brown, Dolores Black, Abby Day and Phil Race, 1998).

Contemporary TESOL is moving towards breaking down unproductive barriers which may exist between teaching and research. We offer some suggestions on 'Action Research' that may alert you to ways that you can continue to do creative research during your teaching.

We then offer some suggestions on starting and building your own teaching portfolio. In many cultures and institutions there is a growing tendency to ask teachers to build up a formal record of teaching achievement. A valuable instrument for assessment of teaching competence is proving to be the teaching portfolio, collecting together evidence of practice, including observation of teaching. If you commit yourself to the building of such a portfolio as a developmental process, you will have an ideal location in which to express the findings of your action research projects. We hope that our suggestions will help you to build your portfolio, so that it is available for assessment if and when you need it.

The remainder of this chapter is about survival rather than professional development, but can be viewed optimistically as 'personal development'. We start with some suggestions on time management. If you already manage your time really well, you are less likely to need our next set of suggestions on stress, but stress is by no means confined to the consequences of failed time management. Then the following set of suggestions is directed particularly to part-time teachers, whose conditions of employment can in themselves cause various kinds of stress. We end with some hints on what to do with the paper mountain that may have accumulated on your desk while you were reading this chapter!

43

Using professional journals

In our field there are a number of journals whose articles are mainly written from the perspective of classroom practice. Such articles can be a useful stimulus for professional development at any stage of a career. The following suggestions should help you make the most of them.

1   **Get access, for yourself and others.** Think both of the international prac-titioners' journals (eg, ELT Journal, English Teaching Professional, Forum, TESOL journal), and of local journals which may be produced by teach-ers' associations in your area. Then find out where they are stocked. If your own institution does not subscribe to them, perhaps there is a nearby academic library which does. Within the limits of copyright regulations, you and colleagues can build up a resource bank of photocopied articles to keep in your staffroom.

2   **Look out for different types of article.** Lots of articles in these journals are 'how to' articles: reports of ideas that have worked well in the classroom for the writer, and that readers could try. But other articles are evaluations of, for example, textbooks, discussions of difficult issues in the profession, or discussions of the rationale for a particular approach. These various article types can be useful in different ways.

3   **Read critically.** Articles are of most use when you can relate them to your own experience, and make your own decisions about the relevance of the arguments and usefulness of the ideas. The following tips give you some pointers to look for.

4   **Find the suggestions in the text.** If, for example, an article contains an account of how self-access materials are prepared in a particular institution, then this could be interpreted as a suggestion that readers might try something similar. If you read articles in this light, you will get a good sense of the relevance they may have for you personally.

5 **Look at the procedural details.** Perhaps you want to try out an idea from an article. Has the writer told you enough about their context and the processes they went through to enable you to see what you yourself should do? What gaps do you need to fill in? Write down an action plan, adapting the writer's ideas to your own circumstances.

6 **Check the setting for the article.** What does the writer tell you about the learners, institution or country that they have in mind as they write their article? Is the writer's situation similar to yours, or different? Can you identify with it even if you have no direct experience of it? What are the implications of any differences between your situation and that of the writer?

7 **Think about the scope of the article.** For example, if the writer is talking about a difficult issue, do they see it as difficult in every context, or just in some? What are the sources of the writer's information about the difficulties? Do you agree that the problem discussed is really there?

8 **Notice how the writer talks about the rest of the profession.** Many articles include statements about where TESOL is at – this, of course, is the writer's interpretation of where we are at. Do you agree with the writer's assertions and implications about what 'most of' our profession says or does? If not, how does this affect your view of the writer's own ideas?

9 **Look for positive evaluations.** The writer will probably tell you that their analysis has proved useful, or that their classroom idea worked well. But do they tell you about the evidence for these claims? What exactly are their criteria for success? Try to find this information, and use it to carry on thinking about the article's relevance for your situation.

10 **Write an article yourself.** If you read a particular journal regularly, you will soon get an idea of the kind of contributions it is looking for, and you may be able to use it as a forum to share your own experiences. Follow the journal's Guide for Contributors and ask a colleague – perhaps a more experienced writer – to give you some feedback on a draft. Good luck!

44

Doing action research

Many teachers find that as their career develops they become ever more involved in investigating and theorizing about their practice and its relationships to the world. Action research is a powerful method for this investigation and theorizing. The following suggestions – the first twelve of which form a sequential plan for an action research project – should help you to consider whether you would like to undertake this kind of work.

1   **Critically examine your situation.** Action research is research with an interventionist goal – its ultimate purpose is to improve what goes on in a classroom and institution. So, the first step is to consider your context in order to find areas which may benefit from investigation and change.

2   **Critically examine your practice.** Action research is investigation into the researcher's own practice. You should narrow down your thoughts about your situation and focus on aspects of your own role within it. What would you like to change about the way you work? What is it in your power to change?

3   **Try to get some colleagues interested.** If two or three of you can engage in action research at the same time, you will be able to give each other invaluable stimulation and support. You can help each other clarify your thoughts about the subject of your research, and use each other to think through the likely implications of any strategies that you plan.

4   **Find a starting point for research.** You should choose an area of practical concern within your day-to-day work, which you think it is feasible to investigate within a short time frame, and where you have a reasonable chance of effecting some change. Think about how you will collect, and analyse, the data for your investigation – the workload needs to be manageable.

5   **Consider your starting point more carefully.** Try to get other perspectives on what is going on, in order to deepen your understanding of the situation. This early information gathering and reflection may lead you to modify your research question.

6   **Get permission to undertake the research.** If you are collecting data, it is essential that everyone involved knows what is going on and agrees. For example, if you are going to record your class, get your learners' agreement first.

7   **Start collecting data.** Depending on your research question, you may take recordings of your classes, interview learners or colleagues, keep a diary, administer questionnaires. All of these research methods have their own complexities, and you will need to read up on your chosen approach.

8   **Study your data.** What does it contribute to your understanding of the situation you are focusing on? Ideally, it will clarify your understanding to the point where you start to get ideas for action strategies.

9   **Plan an action strategy.** In the light of the understanding you have gained from your investigation, formulate a strategy to improve matters. You will need to think through all the likely implications of your chosen strategy, and may have to gain the agreement of others before you can carry it out.

10   **Act, record and reflect.** As you carry out your strategy, you should record what happens – you could use a diary, tape recordings, interviews, etc. These sources of data will allow you to reflect on how your strategy is working.

11   **Continue the cycle of action and reflection.** Your strategies will certainly change things; equally certain, they will not 'solve' the original problem completely. The results of your strategy will contribute to your evolving understanding of your situation and may – depending on the time you have available for the project – suggest further action strategies which can be evaluated in their turn.

12   **Make your research public.** There are many ways of doing this, informally or formally. On a scale of informal to formal, there are options such as: talking to colleagues who are also doing action research; reporting to a larger teachers' meeting; giving a conference paper; writing an article. The important thing is to find a way of sharing what you have learnt.

13 **Read up on action research.** The suggestions on these pages have barely scratched the surface of what you can do – they include little procedural detail and even fewer considerations of underlying issues . But they may have awakened your interest – if so, then before you start work read one of the many books or articles available on classroom action research. This will help you to plan a really good project.

45

Starting a teaching portfolio

To start, and build, a teaching portfolio is potentially a rich developmental process, helping you to understand more about how you teach and which aspects of your practice are most satisfactory. It is also one of the most successful ways of demonstrating teaching quality. In many countries, attention is being given, in educational institutions, to the importance of evidence of the quality of teaching as a consideration for appointment to teaching posts and for promotion. The following suggestions should help you to go about building up a representative portfolio of your work.

1   **Decide *why* you want to build a teaching portfolio.** It is best that you *want* to build one, rather than simply that someone else has asked you to build one. If you are committed to continue to develop as a teacher, a portfolio can be a valuable record of the work you undertake as part of this process. It can also be useful evidence of the quality of your work with learners when you apply for promotion, or when you apply for new teaching posts elsewhere. It can also be a valuable discussion vehicle for appraisal interviews.

2   **Check whether your institution already has specific criteria for a teaching portfolio.** Some institutions operate 'Teaching Fellowships', or similar schemes, and have already spelled out the nature of a teaching portfolio. If a framework already exists, you should keep it firmly in mind, both while collecting data and annotating it with your own reflective commentaries.

3   **Start collecting data straightaway.** Much of the content of your teaching portfolio will come from your everyday work with learners. The most efficient way of starting off a teaching portfolio is to decide what sort of data will be useful, and start collecting examples of this data as a normal part of your everyday work.

4   **Decide what sort of data you will need.** The exact nature of your own data will depend upon the kind of work you do with learners in your job. Make a list of the main things that you do in your job, and alongside each of these write down a few words about the sort of data you could collect to investigate the success of your practice.

5   **Collect data on your course and syllabus design work.** This can include examples of a course area you have planned, intended learning outcomes or objectives you have formulated or adapted, and plans for how you structure your delivery of a syllabus area. You can also include changes you make to existing programmes, with your rationale and justification for such changes.

6   **Collect data on your teaching itself.** This can include examples of lesson plans, course plans and the materials that you use in your teaching, such as handout materials, overhead transparencies and other learning resources that you devise or adapt. You can also include examples of video recordings of actual teaching sessions, ranging from whole class sessions to one-to-one encounters with learners. Remember to be highly selective! A good teaching portfolio includes many *kinds* of data, but only a few examples of each kind.

7   **Collect data from learner feedback on your teaching.** This can include examples of feedback questionnaires completed by learners, along with your own analysis of the overall findings from the feedback. Include reflective comments about changes that you have made, or will make, as a result of feedback from learners.

8   **Collect data from your feedback *to* learners.** This can include photocopies of typical assessed work, showing how you give learners feedback on their written work. You can also include assignment return sheets that you have devised, and an account of other ways that you ensure that learners receive feedback on their progress and performance.

9   **Collect data on your assessment work.** This can include examples of tests and exercises that you set learners, and a breakdown of how each test performed in practice. It is useful to link the content of each of the tests and exercises to the intended learning outcomes, as expressed in the syllabus areas that you are working within.

10   **Collect data on other important aspects of your work.** Such areas can include your participation in course teams, committees and assessment boards. You can also include data relating to work you undertake jointly with other staff, to look at how well you can work with colleagues.

11　**File your data systematically.** Don't put it all in a file or a drawer! Sort it first, according to the particular sections of your portfolio that the data will go into. It is worth starting up a number of parallel files, to make sure you make it easy to decide where each element of your data should be stored.

46

Building your teaching portfolio

Having a well-filed collection of data relating to your teaching is a good start towards assembling your actual teaching portfolio. The danger is that analysing it and putting it all together seems like an enormous task, and tends not to get started! The following suggestions should help you to make the task of building your portfolio more straightforward, as a step-by-step process.

1   **Decide on the physical form of your portfolio.** For example, you may decide to use a ring binder or lever-arch file. Such formats make it much easier to adjust the contents of your portfolio, or to rearrange the order in which you present sections. They also allow you to use punched, plastic wallets to collect together samples of papers such as feedback questionnaires, marked learner work, and so on.

2   **Be really clear about *primary* data and *secondary* data.** For the purposes of your portfolio, it is worth defining primary data as the reflective bits that you write about your own teaching, and secondary data as the backup for your claims and comments in your primary data. Much of the material that you have systematically filed will be the source from which you select your secondary data, while the primary data will largely be written as you start to work on the portfolio itself.

3   **Turn your secondary data into appendices.** Each of these will contain selected examples of data about your teaching. Separate appendices could contain respectively such things as handouts, lists of intended learning outcomes, examples of your feedback to learners, examples of feedback to you from learners, examples of assessed tasks that you have designed and used, and so on. Be very selective regarding the data you include in these appendices. It is much better that the appendices collectively cover a wide range of different data, than many examples of one kind of data.

4   **Make a draft index.** Decide in which order you wish to present data and reflections. There is no 'right' order; it will depend on the nature of your work, and the range of data you wish to present. It is, however, very useful to have this order sorted out in your mind before you start to put together the 'front-end' of your portfolio, in other words, your reflections and commentaries arising from your secondary data.

5   **Think of your target audience.** Who is going to read your portfolio? More importantly, who will perhaps make judgements on it? The people who are most likely to look at it in detail are those whose responsibility includes teaching quality.

6   **Put TESOL into perspective.** Those reading your portfolio for (for example) promotion purposes may not be professionals in the area of TESOL. In such cases, it could be useful to include, near the start of your portfolio, an element which explains (very concisely, and without TESOL jargon) the special aspects and problems of teaching, learning and assessment in the TESOL discipline.

7   **Don't write the introduction yet!** The introduction to a portfolio is extremely important. There is no second chance to make a good first impression! You can only write a really good introduction when you know exactly what you're introducing, so leave the introduction until you've more or less finished everything else in your portfolio. You can, of course, write a *draft* introduction, but this is probably best as a bullet-point list, or a mindmap sketch.

8   **Write (or polish) the reflective pieces *about* each section of secondary data.** You may already have written some of these, such as your analysis of learner feedback on a course, or your discussion of the planning of the learning outcomes for a new course element. However, now is the time to make sure that all of these 'primary' parts of your portfolio will hang together nicely, and will be written in the same overall style and voice.

9   **Get other people's feedback.** Another pair of eyes is always useful. Show bits of your portfolio to colleagues, friends and contacts in other institutions if you can. Ask them to scribble liberally over anything where it could be worth you having second thoughts, or further explanations. Also ask them also not to hesitate in pointing out typographical or grammatical errors: it is always easier for someone else to find them than for us to spot our own!

10   **Now write the introduction.** It also helps enormously to present first a good contents page, based on the draft index you started out with. Try to make sure that your portfolio is easy for any reader to navigate. Make it easy for your readers to tell the difference between your primary data, and the backup examples that are there as supporting data. It is normally better to collect together all of the primary data (your reflections, analyses, action plans, and so on) at the front of the portfolio, with all of your secondary data (illustrating your work in teaching, learning, and assessment) thereafter. This makes it clear that your readers are intended to *read* the primary data and *scan* the secondary data, especially if they have limited time to give to your portfolio.

47

Managing your time

Time management skills are not only connected with effectiveness and efficiency, but are closely related to the quality of your life. Stress is less likely to be associated with having too much to do, than with the feeling that there is not enough time to do it all in. Often teachers have much of their time predetermined by their teaching timetables and assessment commitments. But even if only a fraction of your working time is under your control, we feel the following tips will help you to make it more productive.

1 **Keep a list of the work you need to do under a series of headings.** These headings could make up a priority list of: *must do immediately; should do soon; may be put on the back burner;* or reflect a four-way split of each item of work as *urgent and complex or important; urgent but routine; complex or important but not urgent; routine and not urgent.* This task list is best drawn up on a daily basis, crossing out or carrying forward items as you tackle them.

2 **Avoid the temptation to do the routine and not urgent tasks first!** They tempt because they can be simple, distracting or even fun. But keep a note of them, they can be done in the quieter patches. However, there are benefits to be gained from spending no more than half an hour on a non-urgent task before starting on an urgent one.

3 **Whichever kind of to do list you use, remember it is dynamic and will need to be reviewed daily.** Time has a nasty habit of moving things on, and what was once not urgent emerges suddenly as something needed yesterday. Remember, too, that you may be better off by doing three things from your list in part than spending all your time budget on just one of them.

4   **Use a wall chart or a 'What I am doing?' grid.** Such devices provide you with a means to plan ahead and schedule your known commitments. They also tell other people about your current activities. It's useful for your colleagues if you also include a location and a note of how you may be contacted.

5   **Keep your paperwork well filed.** It's a temptation just to 'pile' the in, out and pending trays! Do this and you'll inevitably spend ages looking for that vital piece of information or, in despair, assume that it's been lost (or not received). Use a relatively quiet time to set up, maintain and update your filing system.

6   **Is your journey really necessary?** Avoid multiple trips to the photocopier or mail point. Ask yourself: 'Rather than see someone, would it be quicker to phone, e-mail or write?' 'Do I really need to go to such-and-such meeting?' 'Do I actually need to go to the *whole* of that meeting?'

7   **Work out which tasks you can delegate, and do so.** Even with tight staffing levels, there will be clerical and technical support staff. Often such staff are better than you at doing jobs like word processing or complex photocopying. They can be quicker, too!

8   **Each day schedule particular times to make your phone calls and to check your e-mail.** Making and receiving calls and e-mails *ad hoc* across the working day can be time wasting and distracting from other tasks. Invest in an answerphone or 'voice mail' as a way to control, but not to lose calls. Encourage those you phone, but who never seem to be available, to invest in similar technology!

9   **Try the *do it now* technique.** Don't be put off if you can't do the whole task in one bite. Break it up into smaller components that you can and will do straight away. You can eat an elephant, if you do it a bite at a time!

10 **In the end you must decide what kinds of activity have a high payoff or a low payoff for you in terms of your time investment.** You may find that, for you, doing your paperwork by e-mail and phoning rather than writing will have high payoffs. You might find that attending meetings has a low payoff, as may writing jobs-to-do lists!

48

Dealing with stress

Working in educational institutions can be extremely stressful as staff are put under increasing pressure to teach longer hours, possibly in unfamiliar ways, and to spend longer hours on assessment and record keeping. At the same time, your learners may have ever higher expectations. If you don't feel stressed, ignore this set of tips! If you are feeling stressed, the following suggestions cannot eliminate your stress, but may be able to prompt you to some strategies to help you to deal with it.

1 **Don't ignore stress.** There are no prizes for struggling to the point of collapse: indeed, this is the last thing you should be doing. As the symptoms of stress become apparent to you, such as sleep disturbances, eating problems, weight gain or loss, headaches or just finding you are on an increasingly short fuse, try to identify the causes of your stress and do something about it.

2 **Allow yourself to feel anger.** It isn't surprising that people under stress often feel full of rage, which may not be specifically directed. People can become very frustrated when they feel powerless, so it may be worth taking stock of what is and what is not within your control. Anger, once generated, can be directed in many directions, and the most harmful of these is inwards. All the same, it is unwise as well as unprofessional to vent your rage on others, especially innocent bystanders who are caught in the crossfire. Find ways to let off steam that are not destructive to yourself and others. These may include some vigorous gardening or other exercise (within your own capabilities), a long walk or even smashing a few plates!

3 **Write it out of your system.** Some people find it very helpful to write about the issues that stress them and make them angry. This can take the form of a diary in which you record your feelings and analyse the situation, or letters you would like to send to the people who are causing you stress, or other forms of escapist or academic writing to take your mind off the

current situation. Be very careful, however, about the ways in which you use your writing. Try to avoid firing off missives in anger that you might regret at a later stage.

4   **Have some fun.** Look for ways in which you can destress yourself by doing things that make you happy. A little hedonism goes a long way. Think about the things that give you pleasure like cooking, reading for pleasure, going to concerts or having a day of total sloth. Regard these as part of a programme of active stress management rather than as a guilt-inducing interference with your work. You deserve some time for yourself and you shouldn't regard it as a luxury.

5   **Don't be afraid to go to the doctor.** The worst excesses of stress can be helped by short-term medication or medical intervention of some kind. People are often unwilling to resort to a visit to their GP for matters of stress when they wouldn't hesitate to seek help for a physical ailment. Don't let such feelings get in the way of finding the kind of support you need.

6   **Use relaxation techniques.** There are innumerable methods that can be used to help you unwind, including deep breathing, massage, aromatherapy and meditation. It might be worthwhile to explore the techniques that sound most attractive to you and try to use them to help you to cope with stress.

7   **Work it out in the gym.** It may feel the last thing on earth you want to do is to take physical exercise at the end of a long stressful day, but lots of people find it helps them to relax. Join a gym, take the dog for long walks, swim, take up golf, play a mean game of squash or just do aerobics at home to help your body to become as tired physically as your mind is mentally. Find out what kind of exercise works best for you and try to use it as a bridge between your working life and your own time. The time you spend will be a sound investment in helping you to keep on top, (but try not to let your exercise requirement end up feeling like another kind of work you have to do!).

8   **Get a life outside your institution.** Family and friends still deserve your attention, even if work is very busy. We all need to learn to keep a sense of proportion to our lives. Try not to neglect hobbies and interests, even if you sleep through the film or nod off after the sweet course.

9   **Take a break.** Often our panics over time management are caused not usually by how much we have to do but mostly by whether we feel we have sufficient time to do it in. Try to take a real break from time to time, so as to help you get your workload into proportion. A little holiday, or a whole weekend without work occasionally can make you better at coping with the onslaught on your return.

10   **Prioritize your tasks.** Try to sort your work into jobs that are urgent or not, and important or not. Do urgent, important things first and do them well, do urgent unimportant things soon, too, but don't spend too much time on them. You will have a great glow of achievement about having got them out of the way. Block in time for the important, non-urgent tasks, so you can do them most effectively. Review carefully the jobs you think are neither important nor urgent, and either put them in a basket of work to do when you have a minute or are bored with your more immediate tasks, or throw them away.

11   **Talk about your problems.** Actually voicing what is stressing you to a colleague, a line manager, the person you are closest too or even your cat can sometimes improve the situation. Bottling it all up through some misplaced sense of fortitude can be dangerous.

49

Working as a part-time teacher

Many institutions rely on part-time staff to cover peak areas of demand or to give flexibility as student numbers fluctuate. If you're a part-timer, these tips aim to help you to keep a level head while all around are losing theirs!

1   **Learn to live with uncertainty.** The advantage to the institution of part-time staff is that you are flexible and cheap. You are likely to be asked to step in at short notice to fill gaps, and you may not know what is expected of you until the last minute in some institutions. Accepting this, and learning to work in a permanently changing context, will make for an easier life, and will bring its own benefits to you in terms of variety.

2   **Look to the future.** Many full-time posts go to people who have already proved their worth as part-timers. If you're hoping for a full-time post, it is worth doing somewhat more than you may be required to, and winning support from those around you.

3   **Develop a range of flexible activities.** Most teachers have standby series of tasks and activities to give to learners when they are called upon at short notice. Such tasks give you a breathing space in which to get to know the learners and plan your teaching programme more strategically.

4   **Find your way around the institution's systems.** You will probably have to find out for yourself how to get photocopying done, how to use internal and external communications systems, and what to do to get paid. Make a checklist of questions to ask on your first day, and keep pestering people until you get the answers you need to help you to do a good job.

5   **Network with other part-timers.** These are the people who are likely to have a lot of the information you need, as they are in the same boat very often. They can also provide you with good support when the going gets tough.

6   **Find yourself a full-time mentor.** This may be the person that you report to, or it may be another full-time member of staff, who will be able to keep you updated on important institutional information. Such a person can help to ensure that the part-time teacher's perspective does not get forgotten.

7   **Help colleagues keep in contact with you.** Make sure that your home phone, fax and e-mail details are available so you can be contacted when needed urgently. Check internal post systems and pigeon holes regularly, and ask a colleague to post mail home to you over any non-teaching periods. It is easy for part-timers to get missed out if they are difficult to contact.

8   **Fight for the right to file!** Everyone needs space to keep records, store learners' work and file teaching materials. Part-timers often consider themselves lucky to have access to a desk and part of a filing cabinet, but you should argue for what you need to help you to do your job well.

9   **Set reasonable boundaries.** Part-time teachers can often find themselves called upon to work almost full-time for significantly less money than their fully contracted peers. It is especially common for part-timers to be pressurized into coming in for meetings outside their normal hours. You will need to balance a natural desire to be helpful, flexible (and employable), while at the same time not allowing people to take advantage of you. You may also need to check what your contract may say about meetings.

10   **Let people know what else you do.** Many people work part-time because they have other work or responsibilities. By informing people about your other lives, you will help them not to make unreasonable demands in your non-contracted time.

50

Coping with your paperwork

Information overload (seemingly encouraged by the availability of computers), is a fact of the life of staff in many educational institutions. Usually the information flow seems one way – on to your desk! This paperwork may also appear to be not directly related to your own course and learner responsibilities. The following suggestions can help you to take care of this general paperwork.

1 **Perform a crude sorting task on the paperwork.** Most of the paperwork can be safely filed. Some requires action on your part, either in creating your own paperwork or as an item for action.

2 **Prioritize your responses.** Deal first with anything that directly affects the wellbeing of learners and/or colleagues. Deal quickly with financial and budget-related paperwork, too. Student records and assessment returns usually need to be processed by many departments and can have funding implications, so they also should be dealt with as soon as possible.

3 **Use your secretarial/clerical support staff.** Their job roles probably make them better than you at efficiently processing standard paperwork. They will be aware of any protocols about official stationery, house styles, etc. There may also, because of quality monitoring and a growing interest in litigation, be a requirement that all external and student (or student's sponsor) communications be centrally generated and a file copy held.

4 **Keep files, not piles!** Handle each piece of paper as few times as possible. Try to avoid the situation of repeatedly sifting through piles of papers, looking for the particular documents you need. Equally, piles seem to 'lose' the document you want. If you think how long you have spent on occasions looking for a particular piece of paper, you will know in your heart that spending just some of that time organizing a good filing system would have been well worthwhile.

5   **Learn to love your wastepaper bin and shredder!** How often have you kept something to read later, knowing full well that you would never actually look at it again – except to remind yourself that you didn't want to look at it? Allow a decent period of time to elapse and then feel free to 'weed' the files.

6   **Label your paperwork with post-its.** These stand out easily from the papers themselves, and you can write on them short messages to remind you of exactly what you are going to do with each of the papers, and save you having to read them all again in order to work this out. You can make your own colour codes with the post-its, maybe to remind you of the 'urgent', or the 'important', as opposed to the 'routine'.

7   **Use plastic wallets.** These are invaluable for making sure that all the papers that need to be kept together stay together. How often have you spent ages searching for that last sheet which has somehow escaped from a set of papers – or (worse) the first sheet?!

8   **Use alternatives to paper.** Would a telephone call be a sufficient response? Can you use e-mail? Electronic communication is quicker, less protocol-bound, avoids paper and saves photocopy costs.

9   **Save paper.** Use notice boards for things you want everyone in your department or section to see. For non-urgent dissemination, circulate a single copy of a document with a 'pass on to...' list, rather than sending everyone a copy – people who want their own copy can spend their own time making one! Make sure that the single copy is destined to end up in a sensible place at the end of its circulation, either back to you, or preferably in the departmental office for filing there.

10   **Take your paperwork with you.** Paperwork can often be done in odd moments between other tasks, and if you have it with you it is possible to make good use of such opportunities. But don't carry too much around with you; don't carry home more than you could reasonably expect to be able to do overnight or over a weekend. How often have you only had time to look at a fraction of the pile you carried home?

11   **Keep *your* paperwork output to a minimum!** You will earn the gratitude of your colleagues if you don't add to the pile in their in tray: use e-mail or the telephone. Keep any written work short and make it clear what you want them to do with it.

Conclusions

In this book we've covered many issues, and attempted to distil our understanding of the accumulated ideas and experiences of many teachers and researchers into sets of practical suggestions on specific topics. At the end of such an exercise, what are the more general conclusions that we can draw?

Firstly, an emphasis on contextual appropriacy. Whether you are choosing a coursebook, deciding how to treat grammar in your class or setting up computer-mediated learning, the needs and realities of your own local context are the most important things to bear in mind. There is no advice we can give that would be equally valid in all contexts. We can and do make suggestions, but you are the one who needs to select from them and adapt them as you implement them.

Secondly, the notion of learners and teachers as whole human beings. All of our suggestions on classroom management and interaction, as well as materials and task design and use, are underpinned by a picture of the learner as someone who lives and learns in a social environment, and for whom the acquisition of a second language is just one part of their personal development. Our last chapter, on teachers' professional development, is underpinned by a similar picture of the teacher.

Thirdly, the importance of responsiveness to learners and of purpose driven work. Our suggestions are based around a picture of teachers and learners in partnership: each party makes a contribution to the success of the learning experience, but teachers have to lead. This places a responsibility on us to find out as much as we can about our learners' needs and wants, and to bring these into our courses. And all of this while still, in the final analysis, being responsible for those courses.

Fourthly, we should emphasize the concepts of research in teaching and communication among teachers. Research does not have to be formal or large scale: everything that teachers do to find out about their learners' language and learning needs, to look in detail at the language their learners are aiming to learn, and to reflect upon and develop their own practice as teachers, is valuable research in our profession. And the more that we can all be in communication about our teaching, either through informal sharing with colleagues, or through more formal presentations and/or writing, the more the profession as a whole can benefit from the work we all do.

Further reading

Chapter one
Cunningsworth, Alan (1995) *Choosing Your Coursebook*, Heinemann, London.
Graves, Kathleen (1996) *Teachers as Course Developers*, Cambridge University Press, Cambridge.
Nunan, David (1988) *Syllabus Design*, Oxford University Press, Oxford.

Chapter two
Campbell, Colin and Kryszewska, Hanna (1992) *Learner Based Teaching*, Oxford University Press, Oxford.
Hadfield, Jill (1992) *Classroom Dynamics*, Oxford University Press, Oxford.
Senior, Rosemary (1997) 'Transforming language classes into bonded groups' *English Language Teaching Journal*, 51/1: 3-11

Chapter three
Edge, Julian (1993) *Essentials of English Language Teaching*, Addison Wesley Longman, Harlow.
Harmer, Jeremy (1991) *The Practice of English Language Teaching*, Addison Wesley Longman, Harlow.
Marsland, Bruce (1998) *Lessons from Nothing*, Oxford University Press, Oxford.
Ur, Penny (1996) *A Course in Language Teaching: practice and theory*, Cambridge University Press, Cambridge.
Willis, Dave and Jane (eds) *Challenge and Change in Language Teaching*, Heinemann, London.
Willis, Jane (1996) *A Framework for Task Based Learning*, Addison Wesley Longman, Harlow.

Chapter four
Dickinson, Leslie (1987) *Self-instruction in Language Learning*, Cambridge University Press, Cambridge.
Fried-Booth, Diana L (1986) *Project Work*, Oxford University Press, Oxford.
Jones, Jeremy F (1995) 'Self-access and culture: retreating from autonomy' *English Language Teaching Journal*, 49/3: 235-242.
Race, Phil (1998) *500 Tips on Open and Flexible Learning*, Kogan Page, London.
Sheerin, Susan (1989) *Self-access*, Oxford University Press, Oxford.
Waite, Sarah (1994) 'Low-resourced self-access with EAP in the developing world: the great enabler?' *English Language Teaching Journal*, 233-242.

Chapter five

Carrier, Michael (1997) 'ELT online: the rise of the Internet' *English Language Teaching Journal*, 51/3:279-309.

Eastment, David (1996) 'Survey review: CD-ROM materials in English Language teaching' *English Language Teaching Journal*, 50/1: 69-79.

Hardisty, David and Windeatt, Scott (1989) *CALL*, Oxford University Press, Oxford.

Levy, Michael (1997) *Computer Assisted Language Learning: context and conceptualisation*, Clarendon Press, Oxford.

McDowell, Steve and Race, Phil (1998) *500 Computing Tips for Trainers*, Kogan Page, London.

Race, Phil and McDowell, Steve (1996) *500 Computing Tips for Teachers and Learners*, Kogan Page, London.

Vallance, Michael (1998) 'The design and use of an Internet resource for business English teaching' *English Language Teaching Journal*, 52/1: 38-42.

Chapter six

Brown, Sally, Race, Phil and Smith, Brenda (1995) *500 Tips on Assessment*, Kogan Page, London.

Genessee, Fred and Upshur, John A (1996) *Classroom-based Evaluation in Second Language Education*, Cambridge University Press, Cambridge.

Harris, Michael (1997) 'Self-assessment of language learning in formal settings' *English Language Teaching Journal*, 51/1:12-20.

Hughes, Arthur (1989) *Testing for language teachers*, Cambridge University Press, Cambridge.

May, Peter (1996) *Exam Classes*, Oxford University Press, Oxford.

Rea-Dickens, Pauline (1992) *Evaluation*, Oxford University Press, Oxford.

Sengupta, Sima (1998) 'Peer evaluation: "I am not the teacher"' *English Language Teaching Journal*, 52/1: 19-28.

Chapter seven

Altrichter, Herbert, Posch, Peter and Somekh, Bridget (1993) *Teachers Investigate Their Work*, Routledge, London.

McKay, Sandra Lee (1992) *Teaching English Overseas: an introduction*, Oxford University Press, Oxford.

Qun, Wang and Seth, Nicola (1998) 'Self-development through classroom observation: changing perceptions in China' *English Language Teaching Journal*, 52/3: 205-213.

Spratt, Mary (1994) *English for the Teacher: a language development course*, Cambridge University Press, Cambridge.

Wallace, Michael (1997) *Action Research for Language Teachers*, Cambridge University Press, Cambridge.

Index

Printed in the United States
72075LV00001B/44

9 780749 424091